SUPER CHUNKY BOOK OF JOKES & RIDDLES

hinkler

Published by Hinkler Books Pty Ltd
45–55 Fairchild Street
Heatherton Victoria 3202 Australia
www.hinkler.com.au

Cover and section illustrations: Rob Kiely
Cover design: Julie Thompson
Illustrations: Glen Singleton
Typesetting: MPS Limited
Prepress: Graphic Print Group

ISBN: 978 1 7430 8713 8

Printed and bound in China

JOKES AND RIDDLES

How many apples can you put in an empty box?

One. After that it's not empty anymore.

When will water stop flowing downhill?

When it reaches the bottom.

What's easier to give than receive?

Criticism.

What are two things you cannot have for breakfast?

Lunch and dinner.

Where do football directors go when they are sick of the game?

To the bored room.

What kind of dress can never be worn?

Your address.

What word is always spelled incorrectly?

Incorrectly.

What has a bottom at the top?

A leg.

What's an ig?

An Inuit's house without a toilet.

What's the last thing you take off before bed?

Your feet off the floor.

What is always coming but never arrives?

Tomorrow.

What can you serve but never eat?

A volleyball.

What do you put in a barrel to make it lighter?

A hole.

What stays in the corner and travels all around the world?

A postage stamp.

Who was the fastest runner in the whole world?

Adam, because he was the first in the human race.

How does a fireplace feel?

Grate!

What gets wet the more you dry?

A towel.

What's green, has eight legs and would kill you if it fell on you from out of a tree?

A billiard table.

What breaks when you say it?

Silence.

What bow can't be tied?

A rainbow.

Why are false teeth like stars?

They come out at night.

What goes all around a pasture but never moves?

A fence.

What is H204?

Drinking.

What can you hold without touching?

Your breath.

What goes up and down but never moves?

A flight of stairs.

What is big, red and eats rocks?

A big red rock eater.

What goes all over the world but doesn't move?

The highway.

What starts with a P, ends with an E, and has a million letters in it?

Post office.

What is always behind the times?

The back of a watch.

Why can't it rain for two days in a row?

Because there is a night in between.

Father: 'How do you like going to school?'

Son: 'The going bit is fine; the coming home bit too – it's the bit in the middle I don't like!'

What goes up the chimney down, but not down the chimney up?

An umbrella.

How many seconds are there in a year?

Twelve: 2nd of January, 2nd of February . . .

Which candle burns longer, a red one or a green one?

Neither, they both burn shorter.

Which is the longest rope?

Europe.

What runs but doesn't get anywhere?

A refrigerator.

What can be caught and heard but never seen?

A remark.

What kind of ship never sinks?

Friendship.

What cup can you never drink out of?

A hiccup.

What kind of star wears sunglasses?

A movie star.

What belongs to you but is used more by other people?

Your name.

What kind of cup can't hold water?

A cupcake.

What can you give away but also keep?

A cold.

What bet can never be won?

The alphabet.

What can't walk but can run?

A river.

What is the beginning of eternity, the end of time, the beginning of every ending?

The letter 'e'.

What has two hands, no fingers, stands still and goes?

A clock.

Now, my friends.
Keep your eye on the heavy pendulum swinging back and forth... back and forth... back and forth. That is what keeps my clock...
CLUNK

What is there more of the less you see?

Darkness.

What part of a fish weighs the most?

The scales.

What's grey and can't see well from either end?

A donkey with its eyes shut.

What is bigger when it's upside down?

The number 6.

Why don't bananas get lonely?

Because they hang around in bunches.

What's the difference between a joke and a wise guy?

One is funny, and one thinks he's funny.

If a woman is born in China, grows up in Australia, goes to live in America and dies in New Orleans, what is she?

Dead.

What has a hundred limbs but cannot walk?

A tree.

Why did the boy sit on his watch?

He wanted to be on time.

How can you tell an undertaker?

By his grave manner.

If a horse loses its tail, where could it get another?

At a re-tail store.

What goes through water but doesn't get wet?

A ray of light.

What do elephants play marbles with?

Old bowling balls.

Why do doctors wear masks when operating?

Because if they make a mistake, no one will know who did it!

Why is a bride always out of luck on her wedding day?

Because she never marries the best man.

When Adam introduced himself to Eve, what three words did he use which read the same, backward and forward?

'Madam, I'm Adam.'

Why is a ladies' belt like a garbage truck?

Because it goes around and around, and gathers the waist.

Why are good intentions like people who faint?

They need carrying out.

On what nuts can pictures hang?

Walnuts.

What did the dentist say to the golfer?

'You've got a hole in one!'

When a boy falls into the water, what is the first thing he does?

Gets wet.

What happened when the Inuit girl had a fight with her boyfriend?

She gave him the cold shoulder.

What do you call someone who doesn't have all their fingers on one hand?

Normal. You have fingers on both hands.

Why did the girl tear the calendar?

Because she wanted to take a month off.

What did Cinderella say when her photos didn't arrive?

'Some day my prints will come.'

Why did the Invisible Man's wife understand him so well?

Because she could see right through him.

Why can't anyone stay angry with actors?

Because they always make up.

Why did the boy laugh after his operation?

Because the doctor put him in stitches.

If everyone bought a white car, what would we have?

A white carnation.

What is a forum?

One-um plus three-um.

What did the burglar say to the lady who caught him stealing her silver?

'I'm at your service, ma'am.'

Why didn't the boy go to work in the wool factory?

Because he was too young to dye.

When does a timid girl turn to stone?

When she becomes a little bolder (boulder)!

What ten letter word starts with gas?

A-U-T-O-M-O-B-I-L-E.

What did Santa Claus's wife say during a thunderstorm?

'Come and look at the rain, dear.'

When is a chair like a woman's dress?

When it's satin.

What did the mother shrimp say to her baby when they saw a submarine?

'Don't be scared – it's only a can of people.'

Why is an island like the letter T?

Because it's in the middle of water.

Why do we dress baby girls in pink and baby boys in blue?

Because babies can't dress themselves.

What is higher without the head than with it?

A pillow.

If a 7-Eleven is open 24 hours a day, 365 days a year, why are there locks on the doors?

How does a boat show its affection?

By hugging the shore.

What did the buffalo say to his son, when he went away on a long trip?

'Bison.'

Why was number 10 scared?

Because 7 8 9 (seven ate nine).

What do you draw without a pencil or paper?

A window shade.

Who gets the sack every time he goes to work?

The postman.

Here! You've got the SACK!
Why have I got the sack?
MAIL
It's full of mail you need to deliver... it's your job! That's what mail carriers do.

What has no legs but can walk?

A pair of shoes.

What is a prickly pear?

Two hedgehogs.

What do you get if you cross a teacher and a traffic warden?

Someone who gives you 500 double yellow lines for being late.

What is an English teacher's favourite fruit?

The Grapes of Wrath.

What goes around the house and in the house but never touches the house?

The sun.

What is round and deep but could not be filled up by all the water in the world?

A colander.

The more you take, the more you leave behind. What am I?

Footsteps.

When does B come after U?

When you take some of its honey.

What is the longest word in the world?

Smiles, because there is a mile between the beginning and the end.

What has eyes but cannot see?

A potato.

What starts working only when it's fired?

A rocket.

What is at the end of the world?

The letter 'D'.

What happened to the horse that swallowed a dollar coin?

He bucked.

What can you hold but never touch?

A conversation.

What did Tennessee?

The same thing Arkansas.

What's the centre of gravity?

The letter 'v'.

What clothes does a house wear?

Address.

Where does Friday come before Wednesday?

In the dictionary.

What do you call a man who shaves fifteen times a day?

A barber.

If a butcher is two metres tall and has size eleven feet, what does he weigh?

Meat.

What's black when clean and white when dirty?

A blackboard.

What kind of song can you sing in the car?

A cartoon (car tune)!

If olive oil is made from olives and peanut oil is made from peanuts, what is baby oil made from?

Is it easier to break the long jump world record in a leap year?

If nothing ever sticks to Teflon, how does Teflon stick to the pan?

Do they sterilise needles for lethal injections?

What was the best thing before sliced bread?

What does a girl look for, but hopes she'll never find?

A hole in her pantyhose.

Where can you always find a helping hand?

At the end of your arm.

What weighs more, a kilo of lead or a kilo of feathers?

They both weigh the same.

What washes up on very small beaches?

Microwaves.

What starts with an 'e', ends with an 'e' and only has one letter in it?

An envelope!

What did the piece of wood say to the drill?

You bore me.

Which room has no door, no windows, no floor and no roof?

A mushroom.

What's taken before you get it?

Your picture.

OK! Now, everybody smile...
BOOM!
Now, hold still for five minutes! And don't move... or you'll blur the photo!

What gets bigger and bigger as you take more away from it?

A hole.

Why do you go to bed?

Because the bed will not come to you.

What has teeth but cannot eat?

A comb.

What goes up and does not come down?

Your age.

What question can you never answer yes to?

Are you asleep?

What is the only true cure for dandruff?

Baldness.

What was the highest mountain before Mt Everest was discovered?

Mt Everest.

What runs across the floor without legs?

Water.

What has holes and holds water?

A sponge.

What puzzles make you angry?

Crossword puzzles.

What flies around all day but never goes anywhere?

A flag.

What kind of coat can you put on only when it's wet?

A coat of paint.

What weapon was most feared by medieval knights?

A can-opener.

Where were potatoes first found?

In the ground.

How long should a person's legs be?

Long enough to reach their feet.

When is it bad luck to be followed by a big black cat?

When you are a little grey mouse.

Why did the girl buy a set of tools?

Everyone said she had a screw loose.

What dance do hippies hate?

A square dance.

What is a goalkeeper's favourite snack?

Beans on post.

What's the letter that ends everything?

The letter 'G'.

How do fishermen make nets?

They make lots of holes and tie them together with string.

What did one angel say to the other angel?

'Halo.'

What did the egg say to the whisk?

'I know when I'm beaten.'

What does every girl have that she can always count on?

Fingers.

What do you get if you cross a cowboy with a stew?

Hopalong casserole.

What do you call a ship that lies on the bottom of the ocean and shakes?

A nervous wreck.

How do you make a hot dog stand?

Steal its chair.

Why was Thomas Edison able to invent the light bulb?

Because he was very bright.

What's the best way to win a race?

Run faster than everyone else.

During which battle was Lord Nelson killed?

His last one.

What was more useful than the invention of the first telephone?

The second telephone.

What did one tomato say to the other that was lagging behind?

'Ketchup!'

What's small, annoying and really ugly?

I don't know but it comes when I call my sister's name.

What side of an apple is the left side?

The side that hasn't been eaten.

What invention allows you to see through walls?

A window.

What are the four letters the dentist says when a patient visits him?

ICDK (I see decay).

What's another word for tears?

Glumdrops.

Which months have 28 days?

All of them.

What's green, covered in custard and sad?

Apple grumble.

How do you make a fire with two sticks?

Make sure one of them is a match.

What did the little light bulb say to its mum?

'I wuv you watts and watts.'

Where was Solomon's temple?

On his head.

What fly has laryngitis?

A horsefly (hoarse fly).

What did one wall say to the other wall?

'I'll meet you at the corner.'

Three men were in a boat. It capsized but only two got their hair wet. Why?

The third man was bald!

It must be great not having to wear a bathing cap!

Why was the maths book sad?

Because it had too many problems.

What did the stamp say to the envelope?

'Stick with me and we will go places.'

I have ten legs, twenty arms and fifty-four feet. What am I?

A liar.

What did the tie say to the hat?

'You go on ahead, I'll just hang around.'

Who is scared of wolves and swears?

Little Rude Riding Hood.

What did the pencil sharpener say to the pencil?

'Stop going in circles and get to the point!'

What do Alexander the Great and Kermit the Frog have in common?

The same middle name!

Name three inventions that have helped man up in the world.

The elevator, the ladder and the alarm clock.

There are three kinds of people in the world.

Those who can count. And those who can't.

Where do you find giant snails?

At the ends of their fingers.

How do you saw the sea in half?

With a sea-saw.

What's the difference between a nightwatchman and a butcher?

One stays awake and the other weighs a steak!

What's easy to get into but hard to get out of?

Trouble.

What has many rings but no fingers?

A telephone.

What do you get if you jump into the Red Sea?

Wet.

What do you call a lazy toy?

An inaction figure.

How do you make holy water?

You burn the hell out of it.

Why did the traffic light turn red?

You would too if you had to change in the middle of the street!

Why did the bacteria cross the microscope?

To get to the other slide.

What did the little mountain say to thc big mountain?

'Hi Cliff!'

What do all the Smiths in the phone book have in common?

They all have phones.

What is the difference between a jeweller and a jailer?

A jeweller sells watches and a jailer watches cells.

What did one raindrop say to the other?

'Two's company, three's a cloud.'

What did one penny say to the other penny?

We make perfect cents.

What did the Pacific Ocean say to the Atlantic Ocean?

Nothing. It just waved.

Who was the smallest man in the world?

The guard who fell asleep on his watch.

What can jump higher than a house?

Anything, houses can't jump!

What sort of star is dangerous?

A shooting star.

Which of the witch's friends eats the fastest?

The goblin.

Why did the balloon burst?

Because it saw a lolly pop.

Why did the farmer plough his field with a steamroller?

He wanted to grow mashed potatoes.

What's the difference between an elephant and a matterbaby?

What's a matterbaby?

Nothing, but thanks for asking!

What did the shirt say to the blue jeans?

'Meet you on the clothesline – that's where I hang out!'

What did the big hand of the clock say to the little hand?

'Got a minute?'

What kind of music does your father like to sing?

Pop music.

What's the easiest way to find a pin in your carpet?

Walk around in your bare feet.

What did the parents say to their son who wanted to play drums?

'Beat it!'

ıat's the difference between
Santa Claus and a warm dog?

Santa wears the suit, but a dog just pants.

Where do you find baby soldiers?

In the infantry.

Can February March?

No. But April May.

What's the definition of intense?

That's where campers sleep.

What do you call a man who stands around and makes faces all day?

A clockmaker.

What did the key say to the glue?

'You wanna be in show biz kid? Stick to me, I can open up doors for you!'

Where are the Andes?

At the end of your armies.

What did the didgeridoo?

Answered the phone when the boomerang.

What did the first mind reader say to the second mind reader?

'You're all right, how am I?'

What did one ear say to the other ear?

'Between you and me we need a haircut.'

What flowers grow under your nose?

Tulips.

What did the ear 'ear?

Only the nose knows.

Did you know that Davey Crockett had three ears?

A right ear, a left ear and a wild frontier.

Why was the glow-worm unhappy?

Her children weren't very bright.

Why does the ocean roar?

You would too if you had crabs on your bottom.

What would you call superman if he lost all his powers?

Man.

What has a hundred legs but can't walk?

Fifty pairs of pants.

What are the names of the small rivers that run into the Nile?

The juve-niles.

What do you know about the Dead Sea?

Dead? I didn't even know it was sick!

What fur do we get from a tiger?

As fur as possible.

Name an animal that lives in Lapland.

A reindeer.

Now name another.

Another reindeer.

Where is the English Channel?

I'm not sure! I don't get that one on my television.

Statistics say that one in three people is mentally ill.

So check your friends and if two of them seem okay, you're the one . . .

Name three famous poles.

North, south and tad.

How do you make a potato puff?

Chase it around the garden.

What jam can't you eat?

A traffic jam.

If the Mounties always get their man, what do postmen always get?

Their mail.

Why are giraffes good friends to have?

Because they stick their necks out for you.

What do you get if you cross a worm with a baby goat?

A dirty kid.

What's the hottest letter in the alphabet?

It's 'b', because it makes oil boil!

What do you get when you cross an orange with a squash court?

Orange squash.

What's green and short and goes camping?

A boy sprout.

We went for a holiday last year to a seaside town.

It was so boring there that the tide went out one day and didn't come back!

What happened when there was a fight in the fish and chip shop?

Two fish got battered.

What's the difference between a young lady and a fresh loaf?

One is a well-bred maid and the other is well-made bread.

What did the big chimney say to the little chimney?

'You're too young to smoke.'

What did the big telephone say to the little telephone?

'You're too young to be engaged.'

What did the power point say to the plug?

'Socket to me.'

What has four wheels and flies?

A garbage truck.

What's the difference between an oak tree and a tight shoe?

One makes acorns, the other makes corns ache.

What time do most people go to the dentist?

Tooth-hurty.

What's small and wobbly and sits in a pram?

A jelly baby.

Why do artists make lots of money?

Because they can draw their own wages.

When do mathematicians die?

When their number is up.

What is the difference between a bus driver and a cold?

One knows the stops, the other stops the nose.

What did the ground say to the rain?

'If this keeps up, I'll be mud.'

What vegetable goes well with jacket potatoes?

Button mushrooms.

Who steals from her grandma's house?

Little Red Robin Hood.

What colour is a hiccup?

Burple.

Why was the broom late?

It overswept.

How do Inuits dress?

As quickly as possible.

How do you make a Maltese cross?

Hit him on the head.

How much does Uluru (Ayers Rock) weigh?

One stone.

What's purple, 5000 years old and 400 kilometres long?

The Grape Wall of China.

What do you call a man with
a bus on his head?

Dead.

How many animals did
Moses fit in the Ark?

None, it was Noah's Ark.

How did Noah steer the Ark at night?

He switched on the floodlights.

Where was Noah when the lights went out?

In d'ark.

What did Noah say as he was loading the animals?

'Now I herd everything.'

How do we know that Moses was sick?

God gave him tablets.

How did the Vikings send messages?

By Norse code.

Do you know where to find elephants?

Elephants don't need finding – they're so big they don't get lost.

Where are English kings and queens crowned?

On the head.

Where's Hadrian's Wall?

Around his garden.

Who invented the weekend?

Robinson Crusoe – he had all his work done by Friday.

Who is the smelliest person in the world?

King Pong.

Did you hear about the criminal contortionist?

He turned himself in.

Why was the baby pen crying?

Because its mum was doing a long sentence.

Did you hear about the unlucky sailor?

First he was shipwrecked, then he was rescued – by the Titanic.

Can a match box?

No but a tin can.

Why are gloves clumsy?
Because they're all fingers and thumbs.

Why did the snowman dress up?
Because he was going to the snowball.

What happened when the bell fell into the swimming pool?

It got wringing wet.

How did the comedian pass the time in hospital?

By telling sick jokes.

Why did the criminals whisper in the meadow?

Because they didn't want to be overheard by the grass.

When is a car like a frog?

When it is being toad.

Twenty puppies were stolen from a pet shop. Police are warning people to look out for anyone selling hot dogs.

Why does the Statue of Liberty stand in New York harbour?

Because it can't sit down.

What is green and pecks on trees?

Woody Wood Pickle.

What wears an anorak and pecks on trees?

Woody Wood Parka.

What did the waterfall say to the fountain?

'You're just a little squirt.'

Who's faster than a speeding bullet and full of food?

Super Market.

Why did all the bowling pins go down?

Because they were on strike.

Which song is top of the Iceland hit parade?

'There's No Business Like Snow Business.'

What wears nine gloves, eighteen shoes and a mask?

A baseball team.

How do you get four suits for a couple of dollars?

Buy a pack of cards.

Why is the Mississippi such an unusual river?

It has four eyes and can't even see.

What did one magnet say to the other magnet?

'I find you very attractive.'

What did the rug say to the floor?

'Don't move, I've got you covered.'

How do prisoners call home?

On cell phones.

Why do bagpipers walk when thcy play?

They're trying to get away from the noise.

What's Chinese and deadly?

Chop sueycide.

Why is it impossible to die of starvation in the desert?

Because of the sand which is there (sandwiches there).

What did the dentist want?

The tooth, the whole tooth and nothing but the tooth.

Why did the belt go to jail?

Because it held up a pair of pants.

Who were the world's shortest lovers?

Gnomeo and Juliet.

What do you get when two prams collide?

A creche.

What are government workers called in Spain?

Seville servants.

What did the shoe say to the foot?

'You're having me on.'

Who swings through the cakeshop, yodelling?

Tarzipan.

What did one sole say to the other?

'I think we're being followed by a couple of heels.'

Why did E.T. have such big eyes?

Because he saw his phone bill.

What were the gangster's final words?

'What is that violin doing in my violin case?'

What's the definition of minimum?

A very small mother.

What illness do retired pilots get?

Flu.

When is a door not a door?

When it is ajar.

Where do old Volkswagens go?

To the old volks home.

Which trees are always sad?

Pine trees.

When is the cheapest time to phone friends?

When they're not home.

How do you clean the sky?

With a skyscraper.

Why did the bungy jumper take a vacation?

Because he was at the end of his rope.

Who was the father of the Black Prince?

Old King Coal.

Why did the Mexican push his wife over the cliff?

Tequila.

What did the electrician's wife say when he got home?

'Wire you insulate?'

Which bus could sail the oceans?

Columbus.

Why did Henry VIII have so many wives?

He liked to chop and change.

Why did the car get a puncture?

There was a fork in the road.

When does the alphabet only have 24 letters?

When U and I aren't there.

Why are rivers lazy?

Because they never get off their beds.

What do you call a snowman with a suntan?

A puddle.

Did Adam and Eve have a date?

No, they had an apple.

How do you use an Egyptian doorbell?

Toot-and-come-in.

How can you tell a dogwood tree?

By its bark.

Where does Tarzan buy his clothes?

At a jungle sale.

Why did Polly put the kettle on?

She didn't have anything else to wear.

Why do toadstools grow so close together?

They don't need mushroom.

Where did the king keep his armies?

Up his sleevies.

What do you call a boomerang that doesn't come back to you?

A stick.

Where was the Declaration of Independence signed?

At the bottom.

Why does lightning shock people?

It doesn't know how to conduct itself.

What is the easiest way to get a day off school?

Wait until Saturday.

How many letters are there in the alphabet?

Eleven. Count them: t-h-e-a-l-p-h-a-b-e-t!

'Mum, why isn't my nose twelve inches long?'

'Because then it would be a foot.'

How did the rocket lose his job?

He was fired.

What's yellow and wears a mask?

The Lone Banana.

What do you get if you cross the Atlantic with the Titanic?

About halfway.

How much does it cost for a pirate to get earrings?

A buccaneer!

What did the digital clock say to its mother?

'Look ma, no hands.'

What do hippies do?

They hold your leggies on.

How did the octopus couple walk down the road?

Arm in arm, in arm, in arm, in arm, in arm, in arm, in arm, in arm . . .

What do snakes write at the bottom of their letters?

With love and hisses!

Witch: 'When I'm old and ugly, will you still love me?'

Wizard: 'I do, don't I?'

What happened when the young wizard met the young witch?

It was love at first fright.

Did you hear about the vampire who died of a broken heart?

She had loved in vein.

Why did the girl separate the thread from the needle?

Because the needle had something in its eye.

Why did the girl wear a wet shirt all day?

Because the label said 'wash and wear'.

What do you call an amorous insect?

The love bug!

Why did the boy spend two weeks in a revolving door?

Because he was looking for the doorknob.

Did you hear about the girl who wrote herself a letter, but forgot to sign it?

When it arrived, she didn't know who it was from!

Brother: 'What happened to you?'

Sister: 'I fell off while I was riding.'

Brother: 'Horseback?'

Sister: 'I don't know. I'll find out when I get back to the stable.'

First Girl: 'Why are you putting your horse's saddle on backwards?'

Second Girl: 'How do you know which way I'm going?'

Why did the girl cut a hole in her new umbrella?

Because she wanted to tell when it stopped raining.

How do you know that peanuts are fattening?

Have you ever seen a skinny elephant?

What kind of sharks never eat women?

Man-eating sharks!

Why did the boy feed money to his cow?

Because he wanted to get rich milk.

Why did the boy tiptoe past the medicine cabinet?

Because he didn't want to wake the sleeping pills.

My sister went on a crash diet.

Is that why she looks a wreck?

Why did the girl give cough syrup to the pony?

Because someone told her it was a little horse.

Why didn't the man want tickets for a door prize?

Because he already had a door.

Why did the girl have yeast and shoe polish for breakfast?

Because she wanted to rise and shine in the morning!

What does every winner lose in a race?

Their breath.

Why is a scrambled egg like the English cricket team?

They both get beaten.

What are the four seasons?

Baseball, basketball, soccer and football!

What has 22 legs and two wings but can't fly?

A soccer team.

What is the smelliest sport?

Ping pong!

What race is never won?

A swimming race.

Why was the boxer known as Picasso?

Because he spent all his time on the canvas.

What did one bowling ball say to the other?

'Don't stop me, I'm on a roll.'

Why did the runner wear rippled sole shoes?

To give the ants a fifty-fifty chance.

Why were the arrows nervous?

Because they were all in a quiver.

What's a ghost's favourite position in soccer?

Ghoul-keeper.

What do you get when you cross a footballer with a gorilla?

I don't know but nobody tries to stop it from scoring.

Who delivers Christmas presents to the wrong houses?

Santa Flaws.

Hey, Pal, five bucks if you can direct me to Johnson Street...

What illness do martial artists get?

Kung flu.

Why do soccer players have so much trouble eating?

They think they can't use their hands.

Why was the centipede two hours late for the soccer match?

It took him two hours to put his shoes on.

Why are cricket players always so cool?

Because of all the fans.

Why was the chickens' soccer match a bad idea?

Because there were too many fowls.

Why is tennis such a noisy game?

Because everyone raises a racket.

Why is Cinderella so bad at sport?

Because she has a pumpkin for a coach and she runs away from the ball.

Why did the golfer wear two sets of pants?

In case he got a hole in one.

What job does Dracula have with the Transylvanian baseball team?

He looks after the bats.

What do you call a cat that plays football?

Puss in boots.

When is a baby like a basketball player?

When he dribbles.

'I can't see us ever finishing this tenpin bowling game.'

'Why is that?'

'Every time I knock all the pins down, someone calls everyone out on strike!'

What part of a football ground smells the best?

The scenter spot!

Why aren't football stadiums built in outer space?

Because there is no atmosphere!

Which goalkeeper can jump higher than a crossbar?

All of them – a crossbar can't jump!

Why did the footballer hold his boot to his ear?

Because he liked sole music.

Where do footballers dance?

At a football.

What are Brazilian soccer fans called?

Brazil nuts.

Why did a footballer take a piece of rope onto the pitch?

He was the skipper.

If you have a referee in football, what do you have in bowls?

Cornflakes.

What can you serve, but never eat?

A tennis ball.

How do hens encourage their football teams?

They egg them on.

Who won the race between two balls of string?

They were tied.

How did the basketball court get wet?

The players dribbled all over it.

Why don't grasshoppers go to football matches?

They prefer cricket matches.

Why didn't the dog want to play football?

It was a boxer.

When fish play football, who is the captain?

The team's kipper.

How do you stop squirrels playing football in the garden?

Hide the ball, it drives them nuts!

Why should you be careful when playing against a team of big cats?

They might be cheetahs.

Why do football coaches bring suitcases along to away games?

So that they can pack the defence.

Name a tennis player's favourite city.

Volley Wood.

Why was the struggling manager seen shaking the club cat?

To see if there was any money in the kitty.

When do clocks die?

When their time's up.

Coach: 'I thought I told you to lose weight. What happened to your three week diet?'

Player: 'I finished it in three days!'

Coach: 'I'll give you $100 a week to start with, and $500 a week in a year's time.'

Young player: 'See you in a year!'

What did the football player say when he accidentally burped during the game?

'Sorry, it was a freak hic!'

What part of a basketball stadium is never the same?

The changing rooms.

Where do old bowling balls end up?

In the gutter.

Why do artists never win when they play basketball?

They keep drawing.

What did they call Dracula when he won the premiership?

The Champire.

Why does someone who runs marathons make a good student?

Because education pays off in the long run.

What is a runner's favourite subject in school?

Jog-raphy.

What stories are told by basketball players?

Tall stories.

Why was the computer so tired when it got home?

Because it had a hard drive.

Where are computers kept at school?

On their floppy desks.

How many programmers does it take to screw in a light bulb?

None, it's a hardware problem.

How do computers make sweaters?

On the interknit.

What do you get if you cross a computer programmer with an athlete?

A floppy diskus thrower.

Hey, did you see who stole my computer?

'Yes, he went data way!'

What did the computer say to the programmer at lunchtime?

'Can I have a byte?'

What do computers do when they get hungry?

They eat chips.

Where do you find the biggest spider?

In the world wide web.

Why was the computer so thin?

Because it hadn't had many bytes.

What is a computer's first sign of old age?

Loss of memory.

Why did the vampire bite a computer?

Because he wanted to get on the interneck.

Customer: 'I cleaned my computer and now it doesn't work.'

Repairman: 'What did you clean it with?'

Customer: 'Soap and water.'

Repairman: 'Water's never meant to get near a computer!'

Customer: 'Oh, I bet it wasn't the water that caused the problem . . . it was when I put it in the spin dryer!'

Did you hear about the monkey who left bits of his lunch all over the computer?

His dad went bananas.

'Do you turn on your computer with your left hand or your right hand?'

'My right hand.'

'Amazing! Most people have to use the on/off switch!'

How do you stop your laptop batteries from running out?

Hide their sneakers.

'I bought this computer yesterday and I found a twig in the disk drive!'

'I'm sorry Sir, you'll have to speak to the branch manager.'

'I've been on my computer all night!'

'Don't you think you'd be more comfortable on a bed, like everyone else?'

'Mum, Mum, Dad's broken my computer!'

'How did he do that?'

'I dropped it on his head!'

What did the computer say when a man typed something in on the keyboard?

'You're really pushing my buttons, little man!'

Why did the computer sneeze?

It had a virus.

What is the computer's favourite dance?

Disk-o.

What is the fiercest flower in the garden?

The tiger lily.

Is that your stomach growling?
No.... not mine!
NEW TIGER LILY
GROWL
GROWL

Teacher: 'I hope I didn't see you copying from John's exam paper, James.'

James: 'I hope you didn't see me either!'

Have you heard about the gym teacher who ran around exam rooms, hoping to jog students' memories?

. . . Or the craft teacher who had her pupils in stitches?

. . . Or the cookery teacher who thought Hamlet was an omelette with bacon?

. . . Or the maths teacher who wanted to order pizza for dinner, but was divided about whether to have additional cheese?

. . . Or the technology teacher who left teaching to try to make something of himself?

'Be sure to go straight home from school.'

'I can't – I live around the corner!'

'Our teacher talks to herself in class, does yours?'

'Yes, but she doesn't realise it. She thinks we're listening!'

Did you hear about the student who said he couldn't write an essay on goldfish for his homework, because he didn't have any waterproof ink?

Mother: 'I told you not to eat cake before supper.'

Son: 'But it's part of my homework. See – if you take an eighth of a cake from a whole cake, how much is left?'

Did you hear about the cross-eyed teacher?

He couldn't control his pupils.

Teacher: 'What came after the Stone Age and the Bronze Age?'

Student: 'The saus-age.'

Teacher: 'What's the name of a liquid that won't freeze?'

Student: 'Hot water.'

Teacher: 'Can anyone tell me what the Dog Star is?'

Student: 'Lassie.'

Mother: 'Did you get a good place in the geography test?'

Daughter: 'Yes, I sat next to the cleverest kid in the class.'

'Of course, in my day we didn't have computers at school to help us . . .

We got our schoolwork wrong all on our own!'

Dad: 'How did you find your maths exam?'

Son: 'Unfortunately, it wasn't lost!'

Why did the student stand on his head?

To turn things over in his mind.

Never go to school on an empty stomach. Go on the bus instead.

Why was the mother flea so sad?

Because her children were going to the dogs.

How do you make a pair of trousers last?

Make the coat first.

What's the easiest way to get on TV?

Sit on it.

What has four legs and doesn't walk?

A table.

What's brown, hairy and
has no legs but walks?

Dad's socks.

Why can you believe everything a bearded teacher tells you?

They can't tell bare-faced lies.

Teacher: 'Why can't you answer any of my questions in class?'

Student: 'If I could, there wouldn't be much point in me being here.'

How does a maths teacher know how long she sleeps?

She takes a ruler to bed.

Playing truant from school is like having a credit card.

Lots of fun now, pay later.

Why was the head teacher worried?

Because there were so many rulers in the school.

Did you hear about the teacher who locked the school band in a deep freeze?

They wanted to play really cool jazz.

Why did the boy throw his watch out of the window during an exam?

Because he wanted to make time fly.

Teacher: 'What family does the octopus belong to?'

Student: 'Nobody's I know.'

What trees do fortune tellers look at?

Palms.

Teacher: 'Your daughter's only five and she can spell her name backwards? Why, that's remarkable!'

Mother: 'Yes, we're very proud of her.'

Teacher: 'And what is your daughter's name?'

Mother: 'Anna.'

'What are three words most often used by students?' the teacher asked the class.

'I don't know,' sighed a student.

'That's correct!' said the teacher.

Shane: 'Dad, today my teacher yelled at me for something I didn't do.'

Dad: 'What did he yell at you for?'

Shane: 'For not doing my homework.'

'Dad, can you write in the dark?'

'I suppose so.'

'Good. Can you sign my report card, please?'

'Dad, I's been expelled.'

'What? We spend a fortune on sending you to an exclusive private school and you still say "I's".'

'Mum, why do I have to go to school? The kids all make fun of me and all the teachers hate me.'

'Because you're the headmaster, son.'

Geography teacher: 'What's the coldest country in the world?'

Student: 'Chile.'

Teacher: 'If I bought one hundred buns for a dollar, what would each bun be?'

Student: 'Stale.'

English teacher: 'Spell Mississippi.'

Student: 'The river or the state?'

English teacher: 'Jamie, give me a sentence beginning with "I".'

Jamie: '"I" is . . .'

Teacher: 'No Jamie, you must always say "I am".'

Jamie: 'Okay. "I" am the ninth letter of the alphabet.'

History teacher: 'Here is a question to check that you did your homework on British kings and queens. Who came after Mary?'

Student: 'Her little lamb.'

History teacher: 'What was Camelot?'

Student: 'A place where camels were parked.'

History teacher: 'What's a Grecian urn?'

Student: 'About $500 a week.'

What would you get if you crossed a teacher with a vampire?

Lots of blood tests.

History teacher: 'What's the best thing about history?'

Mary: 'All the dates.'

History teacher: 'Why do we refer to the period around 1000 years AD as the Dark Ages?'

Student: 'Because there were so many knights.'

Maths teacher: 'Paul. If you had five pieces of chocolate and Sam asked for one of them, how many would you have left?'

Paul: 'Five.'

Why did the teacher wear sunglasses?

Because his students were so bright.

Principal: 'You should have been here at 9 o'clock.'

Student: 'Why, what happened?'

In which class do you learn how to shop for bargains?

Buy-ology.

Science teacher: 'What are nitrates?'

Student: 'Cheaper than day rates.'

Teacher: 'I wish you'd pay a little attention.'

Student: 'I'm paying as little attention as possible.'

Student: 'Would you punish someone for something they didn't do?'

Teacher: 'Of course not.'

Student: 'Good, because I didn't do my homework.'

Laugh, and the class laughs with you.

But you get detention alone.

Science teacher: 'Which travels faster, heat or cold?'

Student: 'Heat, because you can catch a cold.'

Student to teacher: 'I don't want to worry you but my dad said that if my grades don't improve, someone's going to get a spanking.'

What's the difference between a train station and a teacher?

One minds the train, the other trains the mind.

Teacher: 'Jane, why did you miss school yesterday?'

Jane: 'I didn't miss it at all.'

Teacher: 'That's three times I've asked you a question. Why won't you reply?'

'Because you told me not to answer you back.'

Why are elephants grey?

So you can tell them apart from canaries.

What is the robot teacher's favourite part of the day?

Assembly.

Did you hear about the two history teachers who were dating?

They go to restaurants to talk about old times.

Where do you find a no-legged dog?

Right where you left it.

What type of instruments did the early Britons play?

The Anglo-saxophone.

What kind of tests do witch teachers give?

Hex-aminations.

Simple Simon was writing a geography essay for his teacher. It began like this:

The people who live in Paris are called parasites . . .

Cookery teacher: 'Helen, what are the best things to put in a fruit cake?'

Helen: 'Teeth!'

Teacher: 'If you had one dollar and asked your dad for one dollar, how much money would you have?'

Student: 'One dollar.'

Teacher: 'You don't know your maths.'

Student: 'You don't know my dad!'

Teacher: 'Billy, stop making ugly faces at the other students!'

Billy: 'Why?'

Teacher: 'Well, when I was your age, I was told that if I kept making ugly faces, my face would stay that way.'

Billy: 'Well, I can see you didn't listen.'

How many skunks does it take to stink out a room?

A few.

KNOCK, KNOCK JOKES

Knock Knock

Who's there?

Alison!

Alison who?

Alison to the radio!

Knock Knock

Who's there?

Ahmed!

Ahmed who?

Ahmed a mistake! I think I want the house next door!

Knock Knock

Who's there?

Avon!

Avon who?

Avon you to open the door!

Knock Knock

Who's there?

Abba!

Abba who?

Abba banana!

Knock Knock

Who's there?

Aida!

Aida who?

Aida whole box of cookies and now I feel sick!

Knock Knock

Who's there?

Artichokes!

Artichokes who?

Artichokes when he eats too fast!

Knock Knock

Who's there?

Army!

Army who?

Army and you still friends?

Knock Knock

Who's there?

Aitch!

Aitch who?

Do you need a tissue?

Knock Knock

Who's there?

Arch!

Arch who?

Bless you!

Knock Knock

Who's there?

Alota!

Alota who?

Alota good this is doing me!

Knock Knock

Who's there?

Alaska!

Alaska who?

Alaska one more time. Please let me in!

Knock Knock

Who's there?

Alaska!

Alaska who?

Alaska no questions! You tella no lies!

Knock Knock

Who's there?

Alf!

Alf who?

Alf all if you don't catch me!

Knock Knock

Who's there?

Alex!

Alex who?

Alex-plain later, just let me in!

Knock Knock

Who's there?

Abbot!

Abbot who?

Abbot you don't know who this is!

Knock Knock

Who's there?

Accordion!

Accordion who?

Accordion to the TV,
it's going to rain tomorrow!

Knock Knock

Who's there?

Amos!

Amos who?

Amosquito!

Knock Knock

Who's there?

Anna!

Anna who?

Annather mosquito!

Knock Knock

Who's there?

Adore!

Adore who?

Adore is between us, open up!

Knock Knock

Who's there?

Adore!

Adore who?

Adore is for knocking on!

Knock Knock

Who's there?

Ammonia!

Ammonia who?

Ammonia little girl who can't reach the doorbell!

Knock Knock

Who's there?

Abe!

Abe who?

Abe C D E F G H!

Winter's here, dear!

Knock Knock

Who's there?

Arncha!

Arncha who?

Arncha going to let me in? It's freezing out here!

Knock Knock

Who's there?

Albert!

Albert who?

Albert you don't know who this is?

Knock Knock

Who's there?

Avon!

Avon who?

Avon you to be my wife!

Knock Knock

Who's there?

Abbey!

Abbey who?

Abbey stung me
on the nose!

Knock Knock

Who's there?

Abbey!

Abbey who?

Abbey hive is where honey is made!

Knock Knock

Who's there?

Armageddon!

Armageddon who?

Armageddon out of here!

Knock Knock

Who's there?

Abbott!

Abbott who?

Abbott time you opened this door!

Knock Knock

Who's there?

Acute!

Acute who?

Acute little boy!

Knock Knock

Who's there?

Adder!

Adder who?

Adder you get in here?

Knock Knock

Who's there?

Arthur!

Arthur who?

Arthur anymore jelly beans in the jar?

Knock Knock

Who's there?

Ahab!

Ahab who?

Ahab to go to the toilet now! Quick, open the door!

Knock Knock

Who's there?

Althea!

Althea who?

Althea later, alligator!

Knock Knock

Who's there?

Abyssinia!

Abyssinia who?

Abyssinia when I get back!

Knock Knock

Who's there?

Adair!

Adair who?

Adair once, but I'm bald now!

Knock Knock

Who's there?

Boo!

Boo who?

What are you crying about?

Knock Knock

Who's there?

Boo!

Boo who?

Here's a hanky, now let me in!

Knock Knock

Who's there?

Ben!

Ben who?

Ben knocking on the door
all afternoon!

Knock Knock

Who's there?

Ben!

Ben who?

Ben down and look through the letter slot!

Knock Knock

Who's there?

Bab!

Bab who?

Baboons are a type of ape!

Knock Knock

Who's there?

Bark!

Bark who?

Barking up the wrong tree!

Knock Knock

Who's there?

Butcher!

Butcher who?

Butcher little arms around me!

Knock Knock

Who's there?

Barry!

Barry who?

Barry the treasure where no one will find it!

Knock Knock

Who's there?

Bashful!

Bashful who?

I'm too shy to tell you!

Knock Knock

Who's there?

Bat!

Bat who?

Batman and Robin are superheroes!

Knock Knock

Who's there?

Bowl!

Bowl who?

Bowl me over!

Knock Knock

Who's there?

Beck!

Beck who?

Beckfast is ready!

Knock Knock

Who's there?

Beet!

Beet who?

Beets me! I've forgotten my own name!

Knock Knock

Who's there?

Butcher!

Butcher who?

Butcher left leg in, butcher left leg out . . .

Knock Knock

Who's there?

Bear!

Bear who?

Bearer of glad tidings!

Knock Knock

Who's there?

Beryl!

Beryl who?

Roll out the Beryl!

Knock Knock

Who's there?

Bjorn!

Bjorn who?

Bjorn free!

Knock Knock

Who's there?

Bolton!

Bolton who?

Bolton the door! That's why I can't get in!

Knock Knock

Who's there?

Bernadette!

Bernadette who?

Bernadette my lunch! Now I'm starving!

Knock Knock

Who's there?

Butcher!

Butcher who?

Butcher money where your mouth is!

Knock Knock

Who's there?

Betty!

Betty who?

Betty late than never!

Knock Knock

Who's there?

Betty!

Betty who?

Betty let me in or there'll be trouble!

Knock Knock

Who's there?

Bach!

Bach who?

Bach of chips!

Knock Knock

Who's there?

Back!

Back who?

Back off, I'm going to force my way in!

Knock Knock

Who's there?

Bacon!

Bacon who?

Bacon a cake for your birthday!

Knock Knock

Who's there?

Bart!

Bart who?

Bartween you and me, I'm sick of standing in the cold!

Knock Knock

Who's there?

Bee!

Bee who?

Bee careful!

Knock Knock

Who's there?

Beef!

Beef who?

Beefair now!

Knock Knock

Who's there?

Butter!

Butter who?

Butter wear a coat when you come out. It's cold!

Knock Knock

Who's there?

Brie!

Brie who?

Brie me my supper!

Knock Knock

Who's there?

Barbie!

Barbie who?

Barbie Q!

Knock Knock

Who's there?

Ben Hur!

Ben Hur who?

Ben Hur almost an hour so let me in!

Knock Knock

Who's there?

Beth!

Beth who?

Beth wisheth, thweetie!

Knock Knock

Who's there?

Beth!

Beth who?

Bethlehem is where Jesus was born!

Knock Knock

Who's there?

Burglar!

Burglar who?

Burglars don't knock!

Knock Knock

Who's there?

Baby Owl!

Baby Owl who?

Baby Owl
see you later,
maybe I won't!

Knock Knock

Who's there?

Bea!

Bea who?

Because I said so!

Knock Knock

Who's there?

Bart!

Bart who?

Bart-enders serve drinks!

Knock Knock

Who's there?

Ben!

Ben who?

Ben away a long time!

Knock Knock

Who's there?

Biafra!

Biafra who?

Biafra'id, be very afraid!

Knock Knock

Who's there?

Boxer!

Boxer who?

Boxer tricks!

Knock Knock

Who's there?

Bean!

Bean who?

Bean working too hard lately!

Knock Knock

Who's there?

Barbara!

Barbara who?

Barbara black sheep,
have you any wool ...

Knock Knock

Who's there?

Bella!

Bella who?

Bella bottom trousers!

Knock Knock

Who's there?

Bean!

Bean who?

Bean to any movies lately?

Knock Knock

Who's there?

Cargo!

Cargo who?

Cargo beep beep!

Knock Knock

Who's there?

Caterpillar!

Caterpillar who?

Cat-er-pillar of feline society!

Knock Knock

Who's there?

C-2!

C-2 who?

C-2 it that you remember me next time!

Knock Knock

Who's there?

Cameron!

Cameron who?

Cameron film are what you need to take pictures!

Knock Knock

Who's there?

Cornflakes!

Cornflakes who?

I'll tell you tomorrow, it's a cereal!

Knock Knock

Who's there?

Celia!

Celia who?

Celia later alligator!

Knock Knock

Who's there?

Carl!

Carl who?

Carload of furniture for you!
Where do you want it?

Knock Knock

Who's there?

Chuck!

Chuck who?

Chuck if I've left my keys inside!

Knock Knock

Who's there?

Carrie!

Carrie who?

Carrie on with what you're doing!

Knock Knock

Who's there?

Carson!

Carson who?

Carsonogenic!

Knock Knock

Who's there?

Closure!

Closure who?

Closure mouth when you're eating!

Knock Knock

Who's there?

Chicken!

Chicken who?

Chicken your pocket! My keys might be there!

Knock Knock

Who's there?

Claire!

Claire who?

Claire the snow from your path or someone will have an accident!

Knock Knock

Who's there?

Cologne!

Cologne who?

Cologne me names won't get you anywhere!

Knock Knock

Who's there?

Cosi!

Cosi who?

Cosi had to!

Knock Knock
Who's there?
Crispin!
Crispin who?
Crispin juicy is how I like my chicken!

Knock Knock
Who's there?
Caesar!
Caesar who?
Caesar quickly, before she gets away!

Knock Knock

Who's there?

Carrie!

Carrie who?

Carrie me inside, I'm exhausted!

Knock Knock

Who's there?

Carlotta!

Carlotta who?

Carlotta trouble when it breaks down!

Knock Knock

Who's there?

Cantaloupe!

Cantaloupe who?

Cantaloupe with you tonight!

Knock Knock

Who's there?

Carmen!

Carmen who?

Carmen get it!

Knock Knock

Who's there?

Cows go!

Cows go who?

Cows go 'moo', not 'who'!

Knock Knock

Who's there?

Cattle!

Cattle who?

Cattle always purr when you stroke it!

Knock Knock

Who's there?

Cecil!

Cecil who?

Cecil have music where ever she goes!

Knock Knock

Who's there?

Caesar!

Caesar who?

Caesar jolly good fellow!

Knock Knock

Who's there?

Celeste!

Celeste who?

Celeste time I come around here!

Knock Knock

Who's there?

Colin!

Colin who?

Colin all cars! Colin all cars!

Knock Knock

Who's there?

Cheese!

Cheese who?

Cheese a jolly good fellow!

Knock Knock

Who's there?

Cook!

Cook who?

One o'clock!

Knock Knock

Who's there?

Curry!

Curry who?

Curry me back home please!

Knock Knock

Who's there?

Cash!

Cash who?

Are you a nut?

Knock Knock

Who's there?

Canoe!

Canoe who?

Canoe come out and play with me?

Knock Knock

Who's there?

Dingo!

Dingo who?

Dingo anywhere on the weekend!

Knock Knock

Who's there?

Dat!

Dat who?

Dat's all folks!

Knock Knock

Who's there?

Dwayne!

Dwayne who?

Dwayne the bathtub before I drown!

Knock Knock

Who's there?

Dale!

Dale who?

Dale come if you ask dem!

Knock Knock

Who's there?

Debate!

Debate who?

Debate goes on de hook if you want to catch de fish!

Knock Knock

Who's there?

Dad!

Dad who?

Dad 2 and 2 to get 4!

Knock Knock

Who's there?

Data!

Data who?

Data remember!

Knock Knock

Who's there?

Denise!

Denise who?

Denise are between the waist and the feet!

Knock Knock

Who's there?

Des!

Des who?

Des no bell! That's why I'm knocking!

Knock Knock

Who's there?

Diego!

Diego who?

Diegos before the B!

Knock Knock

Who's there?

Dish!

Dish who?

Dish is getting boring!
Open the door!

Knock Knock

Who's there?

Don!

Don who?

Don just stand there! Open the door!

Knock Knock

Who's there?

Diss!

Diss who?

Diss is a recorded message! 'Knock Knock, Knock Knock, Knock Knock.'

Knock Knock

Who's there?

Diss!

Diss who?

Diss is ridiculous! Let me in!

Knock Knock

Who's there?

Disguise!

Disguise who?

Disguise the limit!

Knock Knock

Who's there?

Diesel!

Diesel who?

Diesel help with
your cold!
Take two every four hours!

Knock Knock

Who's there?

Doctor!

Doctor who?

That's right!

Knock Knock

Who's there?

Despair!

Despair who?

Despair tyre is flat!

Knock Knock

Who's there?

Don!

Don who?

Donkey rides! Donkey rides!
Only five dollars a ride!

Knock Knock

Who's there?

Duncan!

Duncan who?

Duncan disorderly!

Knock Knock

Who's there?

Dishes!

Dishes who?

Dishes a very bad joke!

Knock Knock

Who's there?

Dan!

Dan who?

Dan Druff!

Knock Knock

Who's there?

Danielle!

Danielle who?

Danielle so loud, I can hear you!

Knock Knock

Who's there?

Daryl!

Daryl who?

Daryl never be another you!

Knock Knock

Who's there?

Dave!

Dave who?

Dave-andalised our house!

Knock Knock

Who's there?

Datsun!

Datsun who?

Datsun old joke!

Knock Knock

Who's there?

Euripides!

Euripides who?

Euripides pants, Eumenides pants!

Knock Knock

Who's there?

Empty!

Empty who?

Empty V (MTV)!

Knock Knock

Who's there?

Ella!

Ella who?

Ella-mentary, my dear fellow!

Knock Knock

Who's there?

Ellie!

Ellie who?

Ellie-phants
never forget!

Knock Knock

Who's there?

Ellis!

Ellis who?

Ellis between K and M!

Knock Knock

Who's there?

Elsie!

Elsie who?

Elsie you down at the mall!

Knock Knock

Who's there?

Europe!

Europe who?

Europen the door so I can come in!

Knock Knock

Who's there?

Effie!

Effie who?

Effie'd known you were coming he'd have stayed at home!

Knock Knock

Who's there?

Eliza!

Eliza who?

Eliza wake at night thinking about you!

Knock Knock

Who's there?

Evan!

Evan who?

Evan you should know who I am!

Knock Knock

Who's there?

Freeze!

Freeze who?

Freeze a jolly good fellow!

Knock Knock

Who's there?

Fantasy!

Fantasy who?

Fantasy a walk on the beach?

Knock Knock

Who's there?

Ferdie!

Ferdie who?

Ferdie last time open the door!

Knock Knock

Who's there?

Fanny!

Fanny who?

Fanny the way you keep asking, 'Who's there?'

Knock Knock

Who's there?

Figs!

Figs who?

Figs the doorbell, it's been broken for ages!

Knock Knock

Who's there?

Foster!

Foster who?

Foster than a speeding bullet!

Knock Knock

Who's there?

Francis!

Francis who?

Francis the home of the Eiffel Tower!

Knock Knock

Who's there?

Frank!

Frank who?

Frankly my dear, I don't give a damn!

Knock Knock

Who's there?

Felix!

Felix who?

Felix my ice-cream, I'll lick his!

Knock Knock

Who's there?

Fozzie!

Fozzie who?

Fozzie hundredth time, my name is Nick!

Knock Knock

Who's there?

Gotter!

Gotter who?

Gotter go to the toilet!

Knock Knock

Who's there?

Gladys!

Gladys who?

Gladys Saturday aren't you?

Knock Knock

Who's there?

German border patrol

German border patrol who?

Ve vill ask ze questions!

Knock Knock

Who's there?

Gary!

Gary who?

Gary on smiling!

Just a happy guy

Knock Knock

Who's there?

Genoa!

Genoa who?

Genoa good place to have
a meal around here?

Knock Knock

Who's there?

Goose!

Goose who?

Goosey Goosey Gander!

Knock Knock

Who's there?

Gopher!

Gopher who?

Gopher help, I've been tied up!

Knock Knock

Who's there?

Gorilla!

Gorilla who?

Gorilla cheese sandwich for me, please!

Knock Knock

Who's there?

Guinea!

Guinea who?

Guinea some money so I can buy some food!

Knock Knock

Who's there?

Gus!

Gus who?

No, you guess who. I already know!

Knock Knock

Who's there?

Guthrie!

Guthrie who?

Guthrie musketeers!

Knock Knock

Who's there?

Grant!

Grant who?

Grant you three wishes!

Knock Knock

Who's there?

Gizza!

Gizza who?

Gizza kiss!

Knock Knock

Who's there?

Howard!

Howard who?

Howard I know?

Knock Knock

Who's there?

Harmony!

Harmony who?

Harmony electricians does it take to change a light bulb?

Knock Knock

Who's there?

Haden!

Haden who?

Haden seek!

Knock Knock

Who's there?

Hair!

Hair who?

I'm hair to stay!

Knock Knock

Who's there?

Hammond!

Hammond who?

Hammond eggs for breakfast please!

Knock Knock

Who's there?

Hans!

Hans who?

Hans are on the end of your arms!

Knock Knock

Who's there?

Harlow!

Harlow who?

Harlow Dolly!

Knock Knock

Who's there?

Hacienda!

Hacienda who?

Hacienda the story! It's bedtime now!

Knock Knock

Who's there?

Havalock!

Havalock who?

Havalock put on your door!

Knock Knock

Who's there?

Heidi!

Heidi who?

Heidi ho!

Knock Knock

Who's there?

Hester!

Hester who?

Hester la vista!

Knock Knock

Who's there?

Hey!

Hey who?

Hey ho, hey ho, it's off to work we go!

Knock Knock

Who's there?

Hijack!

Hijack who?

Hi Jack! Where's Jill?

Knock Knock

Who's there?

House!

House who?

House it going?

Knock Knock

Who's there?

Haywood, Hugh and Harry!

Haywood, Hugh and Harry who?

Haywood, Hugh, Harry up and open the door!

Knock Knock

Who's there?

Hugo!

Hugo who?

Hugo one way,
I'll go the other!

Knock Knock

Who's there?

Ice-cream soda!

Ice-cream soda who?

Ice-cream soda neighbours wake up!

Knock Knock

Who's there?

Ike!

Ike who?

(sings) Ike could have danced all night!

Knock Knock

Who's there?

Ima!

Ima who?

Ima going home if you don't let me in!

Knock Knock

Who's there?

Ines!

Ines who?

Ines second I'm going to turn around and go home!

Knock Knock

Who's there?

Iran!

Iran who?

Iran thirty laps around the track and I'm very tired now!

Knock Knock

Who's there?

Ira!

Ira who?

Ira-te if you don't let me in!

Knock Knock

Who's there?

Ivan!

Ivan who?

No, Ivanhoe!

Knock Knock

Who's there?

Ice-cream!

Ice-cream who?

Ice-cream,
you scream!

Knock Knock

Who's there?

Icon!

Icon who?

Icon tell you another knock knock joke! Do you want me to?

Knock Knock

Who's there?

Ida!

Ida who?

Ida hard time getting here!

Knock Knock

Who's there?

Icy!

Icy who?

I see your underwear!

Knock Knock

Who's there?

Irish stew!

Irish stew who?

Irish stew in the name of the law!

Knock Knock

Who's there?

Ida!

Ida who?

(sings) Ida know why I love you like I do!

Knock Knock

Who's there?

Irish!

Irish who?

Irish I had a million dollars!

Knock Knock

Who's there?

Ivor!

Ivor who?

Ivor you let me in or I'll break the door down!

Knock Knock!

Who's there?

Irish!

Irish who?

Irish I knew some more knock knock jokes.

Knock Knock

Who's there?

Jamaica!

Jamaica who?

Jamaica mistake!

Knock Knock

Who's there?

Jam!

Jam who?

Jam mind, I'm trying to get out!

Knock Knock

Who's there?

Jasmine!

Jasmine who?

Jasmine play the saxophone, piano and trumpet!

Knock Knock

Who's there?

Jean!

Jean who?

Jean-ius! Ask me a question!

Knock Knock

Who's there?

Justin!

Justin who?

Justin time
for lunch!

Knock Knock

Who's there?

Jerry!

Jerry who?

Jerry can, even if you can't!

Knock Knock

Who's there?

Jess!

Jess who?

Jess me and my shadow!

Knock Knock

Who's there?

Jester!

Jester who?

Jester minute! I'm looking for my key!

Knock Knock

Who's there?

Jethro!

Jethro who?

Jethro a rope out the window!

Knock Knock

Who's there?

Jewell!

Jewell who?

Jewell know me when you see me!

Knock Knock

Who's there?

Juan!

Juan who?

(sings) Juan two three o'clock, four o'clock rock!

Knock Knock

Who's there?

Jaws!

Jaws who?

Jaws truly!

Knock Knock

Who's there?

Juno!

Juno who?

I know who, do you know who?

Knock Knock

Who's there?

Justice!

Justice who?

Justice I thought! You won't let me in!

Knock Knock

Who's there?

Java!

Java who?

Java dollar you can lend me?

Knock Knock

Who's there?

Jeff!

Jeff who?

Jeff in one ear, can you please speak a bit louder!

Knock Knock

Who's there?

Jim!

Jim who?

Jim mind if we come in?

Knock Knock

Who's there?

Kenya!

Kenya who?

Kenya keep the noise down, some of us are trying to sleep!

Knock Knock

Who's there?

Knee!

Knee who?

Knee-d you ask?

Knock Knock

Who's there?

Knock Knock

Who's there?

Knock Knock

Who's there?

I'm sorry, but Mum told me never to speak to strangers!

Knock Knock

Who's there?

Kent!

Kent who?

Kent you let me in?

Knock Knock

Who's there?

Ken!

Ken who?

Ken I come in?
It's raining!

Knock Knock

Who's there?

Kipper!

Kipper who?

Kipper your hands off me!

Knock Knock

Who's there?

Lettuce!

Lettuce who?

Lettuce in, it's cold outside!

Knock Knock
Who's there?
Lee King!
Lee King who?
Lee King bucket!

Knock Knock
Who's there?
Luke!
Luke who?
Luke through
the peephole
and you'll see!

Knock Knock

Who's there?

Len!

Len who?

Len me some money!

Knock Knock

Who's there?

Leonie!

Leonie who?

Leonie one for me!

Knock Knock

Who's there?

Les!

Les who?

Les go out for dinner!

Knock Knock

Who's there?

Lillian!

Lillian who?

Lillian the garden!

Knock Knock

Who's there?

Lucinda!

Lucinda who?

(sings) Lucinda sky with diamonds!

Knock Knock

Who's there?

Lucy!

Lucy who?

Lucy lastic is embarrassing!

Knock Knock

Who's there?

Lass!

Lass who?

Are you a cowboy?

Knock Knock

Who's there?

Lisa!

Lisa who?

Lisa new car, furniture or computer equipment!

Knock Knock

Who's there?

Lena!

Lena who?

Lena little closer and I'll tell you!

Knock Knock

Who's there?

Larva!

Larva who?

I larva you!

Knock Knock

Who's there?

Little old lady!

Little old lady who?

I didn't know you could yodel!

Knock Knock

Who's there?

Letter!

Letter who?

Letter in or she'll knock the door down!

Knock Knock

Who's there?

Minnie!

Minnie who?

Minnie people would like to know!

Knock Knock

Who's there?

Midas!

Midas who?

Midas well let me in!

Knock Knock

Who's there?

Maia!

Maia who?

Maiaunt and uncle are coming to stay!

Knock Knock

Who's there?

Malcolm!

Malcolm who?

Malcolm you won't open the door?

Knock Knock

Who's there?

Mister!

Mister who?

Mister last train home!

Knock Knock

Who's there?

Manny!

Manny who?

Manny are called, few are chosen!

Knock-Knock

Who's there?

My panther.

My panther who?

My panther falling down!

Knock Knock

Who's there?

Marie!

Marie who?

Marie the one you love!

Knock Knock

Who's there?

Martha!

Martha who?

Martha up to the top of the hill and marched them down again!

Knock Knock

Who's there?

Mary!

Mary who?

Mary Christmas and a happy new year!

Knock Knock

Who's there?

Matt!

Matt who?

Matter of fact!

Knock Knock

Who's there?

Matthew!

Matthew who?

Matthew lace has come undone!

Knock Knock

Who's there?

Miniature!

Miniature who?

Miniature let me in I'll tell you!

Knock Knock

Who's there?

Mayonnaise!

Mayonnaise who?

Mayonnaise are hurting!
I think I need glasses!

Knock Knock

Who's there?

Meg!

Meg who?

Meg up your own mind!

Knock Knock

Who's there?

Mickey!

Mickey who?

Mickey is stuck in the lock!

Knock Knock

Who's there?

Mike and Angelo!

Mike and Angelo who?

Mike and Angelo was a great sculptor!

Knock Knock

Who's there?

Moppet!

Moppet who?

Moppet up before someone slips!

Knock Knock

Who's there?

Mortimer!

Mortimer who?

Mortimer than meets the eyes!

Knock Knock

Who's there?

Madam!

Madam who?

Madam foot got stuck in the door!

Knock Knock

Who's there?

Mandy!

Mandy who?

Mandy lifeboats, we're sinking!

Knock Knock

Who's there?

Mabel!

Mabel who?

Mabel doesn't work either!

Knock Knock

Who's there?

Noah!

Noah who?

Noah good place for a meal?

Knock Knock

Who's there?

Norma Lee!

Norma Lee who?

Norma Lee I'd be at school but I've got the day off!

Knock Knock

Who's there?

Noah!

Noah who?

Noah counting for taste!

Knock Knock

Who's there?

Noah!

Noah who?

Noah yes? What's your decision?

Knock Knock

Who's there?

Noise!

Noise who?

Noise to see you!

Knock Knock

Who's there?

Norway!

Norway who?

Norway am I leaving until
I've spoken to you!

Knock Knock

Who's there?

Nanna!

Nanna who?

Nanna your business!

Knock Knock

Who's there?

Nose!

Nose who?

Nosey parker! Mind your own business!

Knock Knock

Who's there?

Neil!

Neil who?

Neil down and take a look!

Knock Knock

Who's there?

Nicholas!

Nicholas who?

Nicholas girls shouldn't climb trees!

Knock Knock

Who's there?

Nobody!

Nobody who?

No body, just a skeleton!

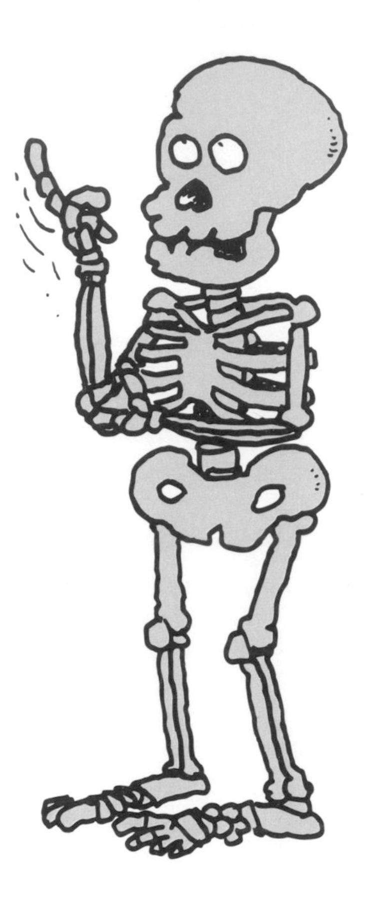

Knock Knock

Who's there?

Orson!

Orson who?

Orson cart!

Knock Knock

Who's there?

Oboe!

Oboe who?

Oboe, I've got the wrong house!

Knock Knock

Who's there?

Olive!

Olive who?

Olive you!

Knock Knock

Who's there?

Offer!

Offer who?

Offer gotten who I am!

Knock Knock

Who's there?

Olive!

Olive who?

Olive in that house across the road!

Knock Knock

Who's there?

Oscar!

Oscar who?

Oscar silly question, get a silly answer!

Knock Knock

Who's there?

Ooze!

Ooze who?

Ooze in charge around here?

Knock Knock

Who's there?

Ocelot!

Ocelot who?

Ocelot of questions, don't you?

Knock Knock

Who's there?

Ogre!

Ogre who?

Ogre the hill and far away!

Knock Knock

Who's there?

Onya!

Onya who?

Onya marks, get set, go!

Knock Knock

Who's there?

Phyllis!

Phyllis who?

Phyllis a glass of water will you!

Knock Knock

Who's there?

Passion!

Passion who?

Just passion by and I thought
I'd say hello!

Knock Knock

Who's there?

Patrick!

Patrick who?

Patricked me into coming over!

Knock Knock

Who's there?

P!

P who?

P nuts, P nuts, get your fresh P nuts!

Knock Knock

Who's there?

Paine!

Paine who?

Paine in my stomach! I need some medicine!

Knock Knock

Who's there?

Police!

Police who?

Police let me in!

Knock Knock

Who's there?

Pa!

Pa who?

Pa-don me! Can I come in?

Knock Knock

Who's there?

Pa!

Pa who?

Pa-tridge in a pear tree!

Knock Knock

Who's there?

Parish!

Parish who?

Parish is the capital of France!

Knock Knock

Who's there?

Parsley!

Parsley who?

Parsley mustard please!

Knock Knock

Who's there?

Pasture!

Pasture who?

Pasture bedtime, isn't it?

Knock Knock

Who's there?

Patty!

Patty who?

Patty cake, patty cake, baker's man!

Knock Knock

Who's there?

Paul!

Paul who?

Paul thing! Let me in and I'll comfort you!

Knock Knock

Who's there?

Packer!

Packer who?

Packer your troubles in your old kit bag!

Knock Knock

Who's there?

Pencil!

Pencil who?

Pencil fall down if you don't wear a belt!

Knock Knock

Who's there?

Paula!

Paula who?

Paula nother one! It's got bells on it!

Knock Knock

Who's there?

Pear!

Pear who?

Pear of freeloaders out here wanting some dinner!

Knock Knock

Who's there?

Pecan!

Pecan who?

Pecan someone your own size!

Knock Knock

Who's there?

Percy!

Percy who?

Percy vere and you'll go a long way!

Knock Knock

Who's there?

Poker!

Poker who?

Poker and see if she'll wake up!

Knock Knock

Who's there?

Phony!

Phony who?

Phony I'd known you wouldn't let me in, I'd never have come!

Knock Knock

Who's there?

Pier!

Pier who?

Pier through the peephole and you'll see!

Knock Knock

Who's there?

Pinza!

Pinza who?

Pinza needles!

Knock Knock

Who's there?

Polly!

Polly who?

Polly put the kettle on! I'm dying for a cup of tea!

Knock Knock

Who's there?

Phil!

Phil who?

Phil my glass up to the rim!

Knock Knock

Who's there?

Quacker!

Quacker who?

Quacker 'nother bad joke and I'm leaving!

Knock Knock

Who's there?

Roach!

Roach who?

Roach you a letter but I didn't send it!

Knock Knock

Who's there?

Rabbit!

Rabbit who?

Rabbit up carefully, it's a present!

Knock Knock

Who's there?

Raoul!

Raoul who?

Raoul with the punches!

Knock Knock

Who's there?

Reed!

Reed who?

Reed-turn to sender!

Knock Knock

Who's there?

Renata!

Renata who?

Renata milk, can you spare a cup?

Knock Knock

Who's there?

Robin!

Robin who?

Robin you, so hand over your cash!

Knock Knock
Who's there?
Red!
Red who?
Knock Knock
Who's there?
Red!
Red who?
Knock Knock
Who's there?
Red!
Red who?
Knock Knock
Who's there?
Red!
Red who?
Knock Knock
Who's there?
Orange!
Orange who?
Orange you glad I didn't say red?

Knock Knock

Who's there?

Rhoda!

Rhoda who?

(sings) Row, Row, Rhoda boat!

Knock Knock

Who's there?

Rose!

Rose who?

Rose early to come and see you!

Knock Knock

Who's there?

Roxanne!

Roxanne who?

Roxanne pebbles are all over your garden!

Knock Knock

Who's there?

Radio!

Radio who?

Radio not, here I come!

Knock Knock

Who's there?

Sawyer!

Sawyer who?

Sawyer lights on and thought I'd drop by!

Knock Knock

Who's there?

Scott!

Scott who?

Scott nothing to do with you!

Knock Knock

Who's there?

Shelby!

Shelby who?

Shelby comin' round the mountain when she comes!

Knock Knock

Who's there?

Still!

Still who?

Still knocking!

Knock knock

Who's there?

Smore!

Smore who?

Can I have smore marshmallows?

Knock Knock

Who's there?

Shamp!

Shamp who?

Why, do I have lice?

Knock Knock!

Who's there?

Stopwatch!

Stopwatch who?

Stopwatch you're doing and open this door!

Knock Knock

Who's there?

Sancho!

Sancho who?

Sancho a letter but you never answered!

Knock Knock

Who's there?

Sally!

Sally who?

Sally duffer! It's just me!

Knock Knock

Who's there?

Stitch!

Stitch who?

Stitch in time saves nine!

Knock, knock.

Who's there?

Sombrero.

Sombrero who?

Sombrero-ver the rainbow . . .

Knock Knock

Who's there?

Sabina!

Sabina who?

Sabina long time since I've been at your place!

Knock Knock

Who's there?

Sacha!

Sacha who?

Sacha fuss you're making!

Knock Knock

Who's there?

Sal!

Sal who?

Sal long way for me to go home!

Knock knock.

Who's there?

Snow.

Snow who?

Snow good asking me.

Knock Knock

Who's there?

Sally!

Sally who?

Sally days yet!

Knock Knock

Who's there?

Sam!

Sam who?

Sam I am, green eggs and ham!

Knock Knock

Who's there?

Samantha!

Samantha who?

Samantha others have already gone!

Knock Knock

Who's there?

Sarah!

Sarah who?

Sarah nother way in?

Knock Knock

Who's there?

Sari!

Sari who?

Sari I took so long!

Knock Knock.

Who's there?

Satin.

Satin who?

Who satin my chair?

Knock Knock

Who's there?

Says!

Says who?

Says me!

Knock Knock

Who's there?

Scold!

Scold who?

Scold out here, let me in!

Knock Knock

Who's there?

Sadie!

Sadie who?

Sadie magic words and I'll tell you!

Knock Knock

Who's there?

Sherwood!

Sherwood who?

Sherwood love to come inside! How about it?

Knock Knock

Who's there?

Shirley!

Shirley who?

Shirley you know by now!

Knock Knock

Who's there?

Sister!

Sister who?

Sister right place or am I lost again?

Knock Knock

Who's there?

Turnip!

Turnip who?

Turnip for school tomorrow or there will be trouble!

Knock Knock

Who's there?

Tish!

Tish who?

Bless you!

Knock Knock

Who's there?

Tank!

Tank who?

You're welcome!

Knock Knock

Who's there?

Turnip!

Turnip who?

Turnip the heater, it's cold in here!

Knock Knock

Who's there?

Tick!

Tick who?

Tick 'em up, I'm a tongue-tied towboy!

Knock-Knock

Who's there?

Troy!

Troy who?

Troy as I may, I can't reach the bell.

Knock Knock

Who's there?

Theresa!

Theresa who?

Theresa green!

Knock Knock

Who's there?

Tex!

Tex who?

Tex two to tango!

Knock Knock

Who's there?

Thistle!

Thistle who?

Thistle be the last time I knock!

Knock Knock

Who's there?

Tibet!

Tibet who?

Early Tibet, early to rise!

Knock Knock

Who's there?

Tamara!

Tamara who?

Tamara is Wednesday, today is Tuesday!

Knock knock.
Who's there?
Tuba.
Tuba who?
Tuba toothpaste.

Knock Knock
Who's there?
Tish!
Tish who?
Gesundheit!

Knock Knock

Who's there?

Tennis!

Tennis who?

Tennis five plus five!

Knock Knock

Who's there?

Toby!

Toby who?

Toby or not to be.

That is the question!

Knock Knock

Who's there?

Teddy!

Teddy who?

Teddy the neighbourhood, tomorrow the world!

Knock, Knock.

Who's there?

U-2!

U-2 who?

U-2 can buy a brand new car for only $199 a month!

Knock Knock

Who's there?

U!

U who?

U for me and me for you!

Knock Knock

Who's there?

Una!

Una who?

No I don't, tell me!

Knock Knock

Who's there?

Utah!

Utah who?

Utah the road and I'll mend the fence!

Knock Knock

Who's there?

U-8!

U-8 who?

U-8 my lunch!

Knock Knock

Who's there?

Vitamin!

Vitamin who?

Vitamin for a party!

Knock Knock

Who's there?

Venice!

Venice who?

Venice your doorbell going to be fixed?

Knock Knock

Who's there?

Voodoo!

Voodoo who?

Voodoo you think you are?

Knock Knock

Who's there?

Vaughan!

Vaughan who?

Vaughan day you'll let me in!

Knock Knock

Who's there?

Vault!

Vault who?

(sings) Vault-sing Matilda!

Knock Knock

Who's there?

Witches.

Witches who?

Witches the way home?

Knock Knock

Who's there?

Willube!

Willube who?

Will you be my valentine?

Knock Knock

Who's there?

Water!

Water who?

Water friends for!

Knock Knock

Who's there?

William!

William who?

William mind your own business?

Knock Knock!

Who's there?

Wayne!

Wayne who?

Wayne, Wayne,
go away, come
again another day!

Knock Knock

Who's there?

Woodward!

Woodward who?

Woodward have come but he was busy!

Knock Knock

Who's there?

Welcome!

Welcome who?

Welcome outside and join me!

Knock Knock

Who's there?

Wicked!

Wicked who?

Wicked be a great couple
if you gave me a chance!

Knock knock

Who's there?

Waiter!

Waiter who?

Waiter minute while
I tie my shoe.

Knock Knock

Who's there?

Wednesday!

Wednesday who?

(sings) Wednesday saints go marching in!

Knock Knock

Who's there?

Who!

Who who?

What are you – an owl?

Knock Knock

Who's there?

Wooden shoe!

Wooden shoe who?

Wooden shoe like to know!

Knock Knock

Who's there?

Weirdo!

Weirdo who?

Weirdo you think you're going?

Knock Knock

Who's there?

Wanda!

Wanda who?

Wanda buy some cookies?

Knock Knock

Who's there?

Watson!

Watson who?

Watson TV tonight?

Knock Knock

Who's there?

Weed!

Weed who?

Weed better mow the lawn before it gets too long.

Knock Knock

Who's there?

Waddle!

Waddle who?

Waddle you give me to leave you alone?

Knock Knock

Who's there?

Wenceslas!

Wenceslas who?

Wenceslas bus home?

Knock Knock

Who's there?

Woody!

Woody who?

Woody now be a good time to visit?

Knock Knock

Who's there?

Winner

Winner who?

Winner you gonna get this door fixed?

Knock Knock

Who's there?

Who!

Who who?

I can hear an echo!

Knock Knock

Who's there?

Wafer!

Wafer who?

Wafer a long time but I'm back now!

Knock Knock.

Who's there?

Wilma.

Wilma who?

Wilma dinner be ready soon?

Knock Knock

Who's there?

Xavier!

Xavier who?

Xavier money for a rainy day!

Knock, Knock.

Who's there?

X!

X who?

X-tremely pleased to meet you!

Knock Knock

Who's there?

Xena!

Xena who?

Xena minute!

Knock Knock

Who's there?

Xenia!

Xenia who?

Xenia stealing my candy!

Knock Knock

Who's there?

Yah!

Yah who?

Ride 'em cowboy!

Knock Knock

Who's there?

You!

You who?

Did you call?

Knock Knock

Who's there?

Yul!

Yul who?

Yul never guess!

Knock Knock

Who's there?

Zombies.

Zombies who?

Zombies make honey, zombies just buzz around.

Knock Knock

Who's there?

Zeke!

Zeke who?

Zeke and you shall find!

Knock Knock

Who's there?

Zippy!

Zippy who?

Zippy dee doo dah, zippy dee ay!

Knock Knock

Who's there?

Zeb!

Zeb who?

Zeb been any mail delivered for me?

Knock, Knock.

Who's there?

Zany!

Zany who?

Zany body home?

Knock Knock

Who's there?

Zesty!

Zesty who?

Zesty home of Meester Jones?

Knock Knock

Who's there?

Zachary!

Zachary who?

Zachary one more minute
before I get mad!

GROSS JOKES

What's green, sticky and smells like eucalyptus?

Koala vomit.

What is the difference between broccoli and boogers?

Kids don't like to eat broccoli!

Why did Piglet look in the toilet?

He was looking for Pooh.

What do you call a lion wearing a hat?

A dandy lion.

What's the last thing that goes through a bug's mind when he hits a car windscreen?

His bottom.

Why do little brothers chew with their mouths full?

Flies have to live somewhere.

What do you get if you sit under a cow?

A flat head.

What is the soft stuff between sharks' teeth?

Slow swimmers.

Mummy, Mummy, can I lick the bowl?

No! You'll have to flush like everyone else.

What's a sick joke?

Something that comes up in conversation.

Who is the best dancer at a monster party?

The Boogie Man!

What's the difference between a maggot and a cockroach?

Cockroaches crunch more when you eat them.

'I just got a bunch of flowers for my wife.'

'Great swap.'

What do you give a sick elephant?

A very big paper bag.

What's brown and sounds like a bell?

Dung.

Why do petrol stations always lock their toilets?

They are afraid someone might clean them.

What do you do if your nose goes on strike?

Picket.

What does a boy monster do when a girl monster rolls her eyes at him?

He rolls them back to her.

How does a monster count to thirteen?

On his fingers.

Mother vampire to son: 'Hurry up and eat your breakfast before it turns into a scab.'

How do you make a tissue dance?

Put some boogie into it.

You wouldn't want to see what's in this handkerchief... IT'S THE REAL THING!

Little Monster: 'I hate my teacher's guts!'

Mum Monster: 'Then just eat around them!'

Little Monster: 'Should I eat my fries with my fingers?'

Mum Monster: 'No, you should eat them separately!'

Mum, everyone at school calls me a werewolf.

Don't worry about it, just comb your face.

What's old, wrinkled and puts away your underwear?

Your grandma.

How can you tell when a moth farts?

He flies straight for a second.

What do you say when you meet a toad?

Wart's new?

What has two grey legs and two brown legs?

An elephant with diarrhoea.

What makes you seasick?

Your little brother's vomit.

How many balls of string would it take to get to the moon?

One, if it's long enough.

What do you call a crazy spaceman?

An astronut!

What do you call a space magician?

A flying sorcerer!

What's another name for a snail?

A booger with a crash helmet.

What's yellow and smells of bananas?

Monkey vomit.

What's green and red and goes at 120 km/h?

A frog in a blender.

What has fifty legs and can't walk?

Half a centipede.

'Daddy, can I have another glass of water, please?'

'Okay, but that's the twelfth one you've had tonight.'

'Yes I know, but my bedroom is still on fire.'

What's the difference between school lunches and a pile of slugs?

School lunches are on plates.

Did you hear about the two fat men who ran a marathon?

One ran in short bursts, the other ran in burst shorts.

A woman woke her husband in the middle of the night.

'There's a burglar in the kitchen eating the cake I made this morning!' she said.

'Who should I call?' asked her husband. 'The police or an ambulance?'

My cousin spent a lot on deodorant, until he found out people just didn't like him.

Did you hear about the two bodies cremated at the same time?

It was a dead heat.

When the fat man was run over by a steamroller, what was proved?

That he had a lot of guts.

Boy: 'Dad, there's a black cat in the dining room!'

Dad: 'That's okay, Son, black cats are lucky.'

Son: 'This one is – he ate your dinner!'

The cruise ship passenger was feeling really seasick, when the waiter asked if she'd like some lunch.

'No thanks,' she replied. 'Just throw it over the side and save me the trouble.'

If you were making a large omelette, would you use chicken eggs or elephant eggs?

Chicken eggs! Elephant yolks are so bad.

She's so ugly, when a wasp stings her, it has to shut its eyes!

There's no point in telling some people a joke with a double meaning. They wouldn't understand either of them!

George is the type of boy that his mother doesn't want him to hang around with.

Three guys, Shut-up, Manners and Poop, drove too fast and Poop fell out of the car. Shut-up went to the police station, where the policeman asked, 'What's your name?'

'Shut-up,' he answered.

'Hey – where are your manners!' the policeman exclaimed.

Shut-up replied, 'Outside on the road, scrapin' up Poop!'

My dad once stopped a man from hurting a donkey.

It was a case of brotherly love.

Three girls walked into a beauty salon. Two had blonde hair and one had green hair. The hairdresser asked the blondes, 'Did you dye your hair blonde?'

'Oh, it's natural,' they replied.

The hairdresser asked the other girl, 'Did you dye your hair green?'

She replied, 'Oh, it's natural. I put my hand on my nose and rubbed it into my hair.'

An astronaut and a chimp rocketed into space. The chimp opened its sealed orders and, as it read them, it started pushing buttons and programming the flight computers.

When the astronaut opened his sealed envelope, his orders read:

'Feed the chimp.'

What do you get when you cross a vampire with a dwarf?

A monster that sucks blood out of people's kneecaps.

The mother monster asked her son what he was doing with a saw, and if he'd seen his brother.

'You mean my new half-brother, Mum,' he replied!

What do you give an elephant with diarrhoea?

Plenty of room.

A woman was facing the judge, charged with wounding her husband.

'You're very lucky you're not facing a murder charge – why did you stab him over and over?' asked the judge.

'I didn't know how to turn off the electric carving knife,' she replied.

Roger was in a full bus when an extremely large lady opposite said to him, 'If you were a gentleman, you'd stand up and let someone else sit down.'

'And if you were a lady,' Roger replied, 'you'd stand up and let four people sit down!'

Did you hear the joke about the fart?

It stinks.

Someone stole all the toilet seats from the police station. The officers have nothing to go on.

Teacher: 'How were your holidays, Penny?'

Penny: 'Great. My brother and I spent the whole time on the beach, burying each other in the sand.'

Teacher: 'That sounds like fun.'

Penny: 'Daddy says we can go back next year and find him.'

What baseball position did the boy with no arms or legs play?

First base.

What did the first mate see in the toilet?

The captain's log.

Why do hot dogs have such bad manners?

They spit in the frying pan.

Three kids were playing in a park when a genie appeared. The genie said they could have one wish each, as long as they made the wish while coming down the slide. The first kid slid down shouting, 'I want a big glass of lemonade.' The second kid slid down shouting, 'I want a chocolate milkshake.' The third kid slid down shouting, 'Weeeeee.'

What do you call a boy who eats his mother and his father?

An orphan.

What is black and white, and red all over?

A nun in a blender.

What is twenty feet long and smells musty?

Line dancing at the old people's home.

What do Eskimos get from sitting on the ice too long?

Polaroids.

What has four legs and an arm?

A happy lion.

What's green and slimy,
and hangs from trees?

Giraffe boogers.

What do you get if you cross an
elephant with a box of laxatives?

Out of the way.

What's green, has two legs, and sits on the end of your finger?

The boogeyman.

What's Mozart up to now?

Decomposing.

What's invisible and smells like carrots?

Bunny farts!

What's the difference between an oral thermometer and a rectal thermometer?

The taste.

Why did the boy take his own toilet paper to the birthday party?

Because he was a party pooper.

Why do farts smell?

So that deaf people can appreciate them too.

What do you find up a clean nose?

Fingerprints.

Why don't elephants pick their noses?

Because they don't know what to do with 20-kilogram boogers.

Why do gorillas have big nostrils?

Because they have big fingers.

Why did the toilet paper roll down the hill?

To get to the bottom.

Where do lepers shop?

At the secondhand store.

Why did the surfer stop surfing?

Because the sea weed.

What is a cannibal's favourite soup?

One with a lot of body.

First Cannibal: 'My girlfriend's a tough old bird.'

Second Cannibal: 'You should have left her in the oven for another half hour.'

First Cannibal: 'Who was that girl I saw you with last night?'

Second Cannibal: 'That was no girl, that was my dinner.'

First Cannibal: 'How do you make an explorer stew?'

Second Cannibal: 'Keep him waiting a few hours.'

Did you hear about the cannibal who gnawed a bone for hours on end?

When he stood up, he fell over.

How can you help a hungry cannibal?

Give him a hand.

Two cannibals were having lunch.

'Your girlfriend makes a great soup,' said one to the other.

'Yes!' agreed the first. 'But I'm going to miss her!'

What did the cannibal say to the explorer?

'Nice to eat you.'

Why did the cannibal have two plates for dinner?

He wanted a balanced diet.

What did the cannibal say when he saw Dr. Livingstone?

'Dr. Livingstone, I consume.'

What did the cannibal say when he was full?

'I couldn't eat another mortal.'

What do the guests do at a cannibal wedding?

Toast the bride and groom.

Mr Cannibal: 'I'm bringing a friend home for dinner.'

Mrs Cannibal: 'But I've already made dinner.'

What do vegetarian cannibals eat?

Swedes.

What does a cannibal say when a bus load of tourists drives past?

'Smorgasbord.'

What's the favourite game at a cannibal's birthday party?

Swallow the leader.

What was the cannibal called, who ate her father's sister?

An aunt-eater!

Where do cannibals work?

At head office.

Did you hear about the cannibal who carried on the family traditions?

He swallowed in his father's footsteps.

Why did the cannibal kidnap the tourist?

He wanted takeaway food.

Why did the cannibal live on his own?

He'd had his fill of other people.

Why don't cannibals eat weather forecasters?

Because they give them wind.

When the cannibal crossed the Pacific on a cruise ship, she told the waiter to take the menu away and bring her the passenger list!

Mummy, I don't want to go to Europe.

Just keep swimming.

Mummy, Mummy, Dad has been run over by a steamroller.

Just slide him under the door.

Mummy, Mummy, Daddy's on fire.

Quick! Go get the marshmallows!

Mummy, Mummy, what's a vampire?

Eat your soup before it clots.

Mummy, Mummy, why do I keep going round in circles?

Be quiet or I'll nail your other foot to the floor.

Mummy, Mummy, are you sure you bake bread this way?

Just get back in. I can't close the oven door.

Mummy, Mummy, can I play with Rover?

We've already dug him up three times this week.

Mummy, Mummy, my head hurts.

Then don't stand in front of the dartboard.

Mummy, Mummy, I think I have a split personality.

Then clean up your brother's room too.

Mummy, Mummy, Daddy just put Rover down.

I'm sure he had a good reason for it.

But he promised I could do it.

Mummy, Mummy, Daddy's hammering on the roof again.

I'll just drive a little faster.

Mummy, Mummy, I can't find the dog's food.

Don't worry about it. Eat your stew.

Mummy, Mummy, I feel like a yoyo.

Sit down . . .
and up . . . and down . . .

Mummy, Mummy, I have a splinter in my finger!

Scratching your head again?

Mummy, Mummy, I hate my brother's guts.

Just eat what's on your plate.

Mummy, Mummy, what are you doing with that axe . . .

Mummy, Mummy, when are we going to have Grandma for dinner?

We haven't finished eating your father yet.

Mummy, Mummy, I just chopped off my foot.

Then hop out of the kitchen.

I just mopped the floor.

Mummy, Mummy, why are we pushing the car off the cliff?

Shhh! You'll wake your father.

Mummy, Mummy, why can't we give Grandma a proper burial?

Oh just keep flushing.

Mummy, Mummy, why is Dad running in zigzags?

Just keep shooting.

Mummy, Mummy, why can't we buy a garbage disposal?

You're doing a fine job chewing.

Doctor, Doctor, I feel like a tennis racquet.

You must be too highly strung.

Doctor, Doctor, my nose is running.

You'd better catch it quick.

Doctor, Doctor, I'm afraid of the dark.

Then leave the light on.

Doctor, Doctor, I keep stealing things.

Take one of these pills and if that doesn't work, bring me a computer.

Doctor, Doctor, my stomach hurts.

Stop your belly aching.

Doctor, Doctor, I have a hoarse throat.

The resemblance doesn't end there.

Doctor, Doctor, I keep thinking I'm a yoyo.

How are you feeling?

Oh, up and down.

Doctor, Doctor, how can I stop my nose from running?

Stick your foot out and trip it.

Doctor, Doctor, people keep disagreeing with me.

No they don't.

Doctor, Doctor, I'm at death's door.

Don't worry, I'll pull you through.

Doctor, Doctor, I feel like a pair of socks.

Well I'll be darned.

Doctor, Doctor, I keep thinking I'm a doorknob.

Well, don't fly off the handle.

Doctor, Doctor, I'm a wrestler and I feel awful.

Get a grip on yourself.

Doctor, Doctor, I think I'm a video.

I thought I'd seen you before.

Doctor, Doctor, I feel funny today. What should I do?

Become a comedian?

Doctor, Doctor, I think I've been bitten by a vampire.

Drink this glass of water.

Will it make me better?

No, but I'll be able to see if your neck leaks!

Doctor, Doctor, will you treat me?

No, you'll have to pay like everybody else.

Doctor, Doctor, I keep thinking I'm a $100 note.

Go shopping, the change will do you good.

Doctor, Doctor, I swallowed a spoon.

Well try to relax and don't stir.

Doctor, Doctor, I swallowed a roll of film.

Don't worry, nothing will develop.

Doctor, Doctor, nobody ever listens to me.

Next!

Doctor, Doctor, I have not stopped laughing since my operation!

That surgeon always has people in stitches.

Doctor, Doctor, I'm so ugly – what can I do about it?

Hire yourself out for Halloween parties.

Doctor, Doctor, I'm as sick as a dog.

Well, I can't help you because I'm not a vet.

Doctor, Doctor, my eyesight is getting worse.

You're absolutely right, this is a post office.

Doctor, Doctor, the first thirty minutes I'm up every morning I feel dizzy, what should I do?

Get up half an hour later.

Doctor, Doctor, what does this X-ray of my head show?

Unfortunately, nothing.

Doctor, Doctor, this ointment you gave me makes my arm smart!

Try putting some on your head.

Doctor, Doctor, something is preying on my mind!

Don't worry, it will probably starve to death.

Doctor, Doctor, I feel like a bell.

Well, take these and if they don't work, give me a ring.

Doctor, Doctor, I have a ringing in my ears!

Well, answer it.

Doctor, Doctor, every time I stand up I see visions of Mickey Mouse and Pluto and every time I sit down I see Donald Duck!

How long have you been having these Disney spells?

Doctor, Doctor, it hurts when I do this!

Well, don't do that.

Doctor, Doctor, I snore so loud,
I wake myself up!

Try sleeping in another room.

Doctor, Doctor, my leg hurts,
what can I do?

Limp.

Doctor, Doctor, I have yellow teeth, what should I do?

Wear a brown tie.

Doctor, Doctor, I feel like a dog.

Then go see a vet!

Doctor, Doctor, I have a pain in my eye every time I drink hot chocolate.

Take the spoon out of your mug before you drink.

Doctor, Doctor, can you help me out?

Certainly – which way did you come in?

Doctor, Doctor, I dreamed that I ate a large marshmallow!

Did you wake up without a pillow?

Doctor, Doctor, my brother thinks he's a chicken.

How long has this been going on?

About six months.

Why didn't you bring him here earlier?

We needed the eggs.

Doctor, Doctor, I feel like a dog.

Sit!

Doctor, Doctor, I keep thinking I'm a dog.

How long has this been going on?

Ever since I was a pup.

Doctor, Doctor, did you hear about the boy who swallowed a coin?

No? Well, there's no change yet!

Doctor, Doctor, my son swallowed a pen, what should I do?

Use a pencil instead!

Doctor, Doctor, my wooden leg is giving me a lot of pain.

Why's that?

My wife keeps hitting me over the head with it!

Doctor, Doctor, my hair is falling out, can you give me something to keep it in?

Yes, a paper bag.

Doctor, Doctor, my belly is so big that I'm embarrassed by it. What can I do?

Have you tried to diet?

Yes, but the different colours do not seem to make a difference.

Doctor, Doctor, I have a terrible cough!

Then you should practise.

Doctor, Doctor, I keep thinking I'm a dog.

Well, get up on the couch and I'll examine you.

I can't, I'm not allowed on the furniture.

Doctor, Doctor, I feel like a piano.

Wait a minute while I take some notes.

Doctor, Doctor, will my measles be better by next Monday?

I don't want to make any rash promises.

Doctor, Doctor, I keep thinking I'm a fruitcake.

What's got into you?

Flour, raisins and cherries.

Doctor, Doctor, my wife thinks I'm crazy because I like hamburgers.

That's ridiculous. I like hamburgers too.

Good, you should come by and see my collection some time. I have hundreds of them.

Doctor, Doctor, I keep hearing a ringing in my ears.

Where did you expect to hear it?

Doctor, Doctor, what's good for biting fingernails?

Very sharp teeth.

Doctor, Doctor, I have a carrot growing out of my ear.

Amazing! How did that happen?

I don't know – I planted cabbages in there!

Doctor, Doctor, can you give me anything for excessive wind?

Sure, here's a kite.

Doctor, Doctor, can I have a bottle of aspirin and a pot of glue?

Why?

Because I have a splitting headache!

Doctor, Doctor, should I surf the Internet on an empty stomach?

No, you should do it on a computer.

Doctor, Doctor, my girlfriend thinks she's a duck.

You'd better bring her in to see me right away.

I can't – she's already flown south for the winter.

Doctor, Doctor, everyone hates me.

Don't be stupid, not everyone has met you yet.

Doctor, Doctor, I feel like a toad.

Don't worry! We have hoperations for that these days.

Doctor, Doctor, my little brother thinks he's a computer.

Well, bring him in so I can cure him.

I can't, I need to use him to finish my homework!

Doctor, Doctor, my wife thinks she's a chicken.

Do you want me to cure her?

No, I just wondered if you wanted some eggs.

Doctor, Doctor, I have a sore throat.

Open your mouth and stick your tongue out facing the window.

What's that have to do with my sore throat?

Nothing. I just don't like my neighbours.

Doctor, Doctor, I was playing a kazoo and I swallowed it.

Lucky you weren't playing the piano.

Doctor, Doctor, I think I'm a bridge.

What's come over you?

Oh, two cars, a large truck and a bus.

Doctor, Doctor, when I press with my finger here . . . it hurts, and here . . . it hurts, and here . . . and here! What do you think is wrong with me?

Your finger's broken.

Doctor, Doctor, I think I'm a mouse trap!

Well, snap out of it.

Doctor, Doctor, I have flowers growing out of the top of my head.

Don't worry, it's just a beauty spot.

Doctor, Doctor, have you taken my temperature?

No. Is it missing?

Doctor, Doctor, I get so nervous when I drive I keep bumping into things!

Don't worry, I'll prescribe a crash course!

Doctor, Doctor, I feel like a pack of cards.

I'll deal with you later.

Doctor, Doctor, I've just swallowed a pen.

Well, sit down and fill out this form!

Doctor, Doctor, my sister thinks she's a squirrel.

Sounds like a nut case to me.

Doctor, Doctor, I feel like an apple.

We must get to the core of this!

Doctor, Doctor, I feel like a sheep.

That's baaaaaaaaaad!

Doctor, Doctor, I'm becoming invisible.

Yes, I can see you're not all there!

Doctor, Doctor, I'm covered in spots.

Let's not do anything rash!

Doctor, Doctor, everyone keeps throwing me in the garbage.

Don't talk rubbish!

Doctor, Doctor, I'm turning into a wastebasket.

Don't give me a bunch of garbage.

Doctor, Doctor, I'm boiling up!

Just simmer down!

Doctor, Doctor, I feel like a needle.

I see your point!

Doctor, Doctor, how can I cure my sleepwalking?

Sprinkle tacks on your bedroom floor!

Doctor, Doctor, I feel like a racehorse.

Take one of these every four laps!

Doctor, Doctor. . .

You need new glasses.

But I haven't told you what's wrong with me yet.

I could tell as soon as you walked in through the window.

Doctor, Doctor, I'm a burglar!

Have you taken anything for it?

Doctor, Doctor, I need some acetylsalicylic acid.

You mean aspirin?

That's it. I can never remember that word.

Doctor, Doctor, I feel like an apple.

Well don't worry, I won't bite.

Doctor, Doctor, my tongue tingles when I touch it to an unsalted peanut wrapped in aluminium foil. What's wrong with me?

You have far too much free time.

Doctor, Doctor, I tend to flush a lot.

Don't worry, it's just a chain reaction.

Doctor, Doctor, will this ointment clear up my spots?

I never make rash promises!

Doctor, Doctor, I think I'm a moth.

So why did you come by?

Well, I saw your light on.

Doctor, Doctor, I keep thinking I'm a spider.

What a web of lies!

Doctor, Doctor, I think I'm a snail.

Don't worry, we'll have you out of your shell soon.

Doctor, Doctor, I think I'm an adder.

Great, can you help me with my accounts please?

Doctor, Doctor, I keep painting myself gold.

Don't worry, it's just a gilt complex.

Doctor, Doctor, my baby looks just like his father.

Don't worry – as long as he's healthy.

Doctor, Doctor, I'm scared. This is my first operation.

I know how you feel, it's the first time I've done one!

Doctor, Doctor, I keep thinking there's two of me.

One at a time please!

Doctor, Doctor, some days I feel like a teepee and other days I feel like a wigwam.

You're too tents!

Doctor, Doctor, my little boy just swallowed a roll of film.

Hmmm. Let's hope nothing develops!

Doctor, Doctor, I keep thinking I'm a computer.

My goodness, you'd better come to my office right away!

I can't, my power cable won't reach that far!

Doctor, Doctor, I don't think I'm a computer any more. Now I think I'm a desk.

You're just letting things get on top of you.

Doctor, Doctor, my sister keeps thinking she's invisible.

Which sister?

Doctor, Doctor, how much to have this splinter taken out?

Seventy dollars.

Seventy dollars for just a couple of minutes' work?

I can pull it out very slowly if you like.

Doctor, Doctor, I dream there are zombies under my bed. What can I do?

Saw the legs off your bed.

Doctor, Doctor, I think I'm a yoyo.

You're stringing me along!

Doctor, Doctor, I keep thinking I'm a vampire.

Necks, please!

Doctor, Doctor, I think I'm an electric eel.

That's shocking!

Doctor, Doctor, I think I'm a woodworm.

How boring for you!

Doctor, Doctor, I swallowed a bone.

Are you choking?

No, I really did!

Doctor, Doctor, I need something for my temper.

Just wait 'til you get the bill.

Doctor, Doctor, I keep thinking I'm a mosquito.

What a sucker!

Doctor, Doctor, I've broken my arm in two places.

Well, don't go back there again.

Doctor, Doctor, I think I'm a frog.

What's wrong with that?

I think I'm going to croak!

Doctor, Doctor, I think
I'm a caterpillar.

Don't worry, you'll change soon.

Doctor, Doctor, I think I'm a snake, about to shed my skin.

Why don't you go behind the screen and slip into something more comfortable!

Doctor, Doctor, these pills you gave me for body odour. . .

What's wrong with them?

They keep slipping out from under my arms!

Doctor, Doctor, my husband smells like a fish.

Poor sole!

Doctor, Doctor, my sister thinks she's a lift.

Well, tell her to come in.

I can't, she doesn't stop on this floor!

Doctor, Doctor, I think I'm a moth.

Get out of the way, you're in my light!

Doctor, Doctor, how long have I got?

Ten.

Ten what? Ten months? Ten weeks?

10, 9, 8, 7. . .

Doctor, Doctor, how was my check-up?

Perfect. You'll live to be 80.

But I am 80.

In that case, it's been nice knowing you.

Doctor, Doctor, do you have something for a migraine?

Take this hammer and hit yourself on the foot. You'll forget about your headache.

Doctor, Doctor, I ate some oysters and now I'm feeling sick.

Were they fresh?

How can you tell?

You open the shell and look.

You're not supposed to eat the shell?

Doctor, Doctor, I came as quick as I could. What's the problem?

Your lab results are back and you only have 24 hours to live.

That's terrible.

There's worse news. I've been trying to call you since yesterday.

Doctor, Doctor, I get very nervous and scared during driving tests.

Don't worry, you'll pass eventually.

But I'm the examiner!

Doctor, Doctor, I can't feel my legs.

That's because we had to amputate your arms.

Doctor, Doctor, I feel like a bird.

I'll tweet you in a minute.

Doctor, Doctor, I feel like a strawberry.

I can see you're in a bit of a jam.

Doctor, Doctor, I think I'm a rubber band.

Why don't you stretch yourself out on the couch there, and tell me all about it?

Doctor, Doctor, I keep seeing double.

Please hop up on the table.

Which one?

Doctor, Doctor, I keep seeing green aliens with two heads and four legs.

Have you seen a psychiatrist?

No, just green aliens with two heads and four legs.

Doctor, Doctor, I keep thinking I'm a bee.

Buzz off, I'm busy.

Doctor, Doctor, my wife keeps beating me.

Oh dear. How often?

Every time we play Scrabble.

Doctor, Doctor, I think I'm a nit.

Will you get out of my hair?

Doctor, Doctor, I've lost my memory!

When did this happen?

When did what happen?

Doctor, Doctor, I think I'm a clock.

You're winding me up.

Doctor, Doctor, I think I'm invisible.

Come back later. I can't see you now.

Doctor, Doctor, I think I'm losing my mind.

Don't worry, you won't miss it.

Doctor, Doctor, I think I'm turning into a woman.

Well, you are 16 now Amanda.

Doctor, Doctor, I think I'm suffering from déjà vu.

Haven't I seen you before?

Doctor, Doctor, I feel like a pair of curtains.

Well, pull yourself together.

Doctor, Doctor, I think I'm a python.

You can't get around me like that, you know!

Doctor, Doctor, my pig has a rash. What should I do?

Try this oinkment.

Doctor, Doctor, I have jelly in my ear.

You're just a trifle deaf.

Doctor, Doctor, my baby swallowed some explosives.

Well, keep calm. We don't want him to go off.

Doctor, Doctor, I think I'm a computer.

How long have you felt like this?

Ever since I was switched on!

Doctor, Doctor, why are you so short-tempered?

I don't have enough patients.

Doctor, Doctor, my son swallowed my razor blade.

Well, just use an electric razor.

Doctor, Doctor, my wife's contractions are only five minutes apart.

Is this her first child?

No, this is her husband.

Doctor, Doctor, should I file my nails?

No, throw them away like everyone else does.

Doctor, Doctor, since the operation on my leg, I lean one way.

I think you're all right.

Doctor, Doctor, sometimes I feel like a goat.

How long has this been going on?

Ever since I was a kid.

Doctor, Doctor, I can't get to sleep.

Sit on the edge of the bed and you'll drop off.

Doctor, Doctor, sometimes I feel like an onion, and sometimes I feel like a cucumber.

Boy, you're in a pickle.

Doctor, Doctor, sometimes I think I'm a biscuit.

Just a little crackers, huh?

Doctor, Doctor, sometimes I think there are two of me.

Good, you can pay both bills on your way out.

Doctor, Doctor, tell me straight. Is it bad?

Just don't start watching any new TV series.

Doctor, Doctor, will I be able to play the guitar when my hand heals?

Of course.

Great. Because I couldn't play it before.

Doctor, Doctor, what's wrong with me?

Well, you have a carrot up your nose, a bean in one ear, and a French fry in the other. I'd say you're not eating right.

'Can I go swimming now, Mum?' asked the child.

'No – there are sharks out there,' said his mother.

'Dad's swimming!'

'Yes, he's got a million dollars' life insurance.'

Doctor, Doctor, you've taken out my tonsils, my appendix, my gall bladder and one of my kidneys, but I still feel sick.

That's enough out of you.

Doctor, Doctor, I have a split personality.

Well, you'd better both sit down, then.

Waiter, what kind of soup is this?

Bean soup.

I don't care what it's been. What is it now?

Waiter, there's a fly in my soup!

Don't worry sir, the spider in your salad will get it!

Waiter, I'm in a hurry. Will my pizza be long?

No, it will be round.

Waiter, this soup tastes funny.
Why aren't you laughing then?

Waiter, this egg is bad.
Well don't blame me, I only laid the table.

Waiter, there's a bug in my soup.
Be quiet, sir, or everyone will want one.

Waiter, how long will my hot dogs be?

Oh, about 20 centimetres.

Waiter, you have your thumb on my steak!

Well I didn't want to drop it again.

Waiter, there's a fly in my soup.

Yes sir, the hot water killed it.

Waiter, how did this fly get in my soup?

It flew.

Waiter, I can't eat this meal. Please get the manager.

It's no use. He won't eat it either.

Waiter, do you have frog legs?

Yes sir.

Then hop to the kitchen, and fetch me a steak.

Waiter, I'd like my steak burned, soggy chips, and a grimy, bitter salad.

I'm afraid the chef won't cook that for you, sir.

Why not? He did yesterday.

Waiter, I'll have the burger please.

With pleasure.

No, with fries.

Waiter, I'll have the lamb chops.
And make them lean.

Certainly sir. To the right or the left?

Waiter, what is this fly doing in my soup?

It looks like the backstroke.

Waiter, I'll have the soup and fish please.

I would recommend you eat the fish first. It's been sitting around for a few days and is beginning to smell.

Waiter, is there any soup on the menu?

No madam, I've wiped it all off.

Waiter, is this beef or lamb?

Can't you taste the difference?

No.

Then it doesn't matter.

Waiter, please remove this fly.

But he hasn't finished yet.

Waiter, there's a cockroach in my soup.

Sorry sir, we're all out of flies.

Waiter, there's a dead fly swimming in my soup.

That can't be, sir. Dead flies can't swim.

Waiter, do you serve crabs at this restaurant?

Yes sir, we serve anyone.

Waiter, there's a fly in my soup.

No sir, that's a cockroach.
The fly is on your roll.

Waiter, there's a fly in my soup.

That's because the chef used to be a tailor.

Waiter, there's a fly in my soup.

Would you prefer him with your main course?

Waiter, there's a fly on my steak.

That's because it's attracted to rotting meat.

Waiter, there's a spider in my soup.

It must have eaten the fly.

Waiter, this apple pie is smashed.

Well, you told me to step on it because you were in a hurry.

Waiter, this crab only has one claw.

It must have been in a fight.

Then bring me the winner.

Waiter, this coffee tastes like mud.

I can't understand why. It was ground just a minute ago.

Waiter, we'll have two coffees please. And I want a clean cup.

Yes, sir. Here are your two coffees. Now which one of you wanted the clean cup?

Waiter, do you have frog legs?

No, I've always walked like this.

Waiter, there is a small insect in my soup!

Sorry sir, I'll get you a bigger one!

What do you call

. . . a man who likes to work out?

Jim!

. . . a boy with really short hair?

Sean!

. . . a woman with a cat on her head?

Kitty!

. . . a woman with one leg?

Eileen!

. . . a boy hanging on the wall?

Art!

. . . a man with a map on his head?

Miles!

. . . a man with a spade?

Doug!

. . . a man without a spade?

Douglas!

. . . a man who owes money?

Bill!

. . . a man in a pile of leaves?

Russell!

. . . a woman in the distance?

Dot!

. . . Someone who greets you at your door every morning?

Matt!

. . . a man pouring water into a jug?

Phil!

. . . a man with a plank on his head?

Edward!

. . . a girl with a frog on her head?

Lily!

. . . a man with a seagull on his head?

Cliff!

. . . a man with a large black and blue mark on his leg?

Bruce!

. . . a man with a licence plate on his head?

Reg!

. . . a man with a stamp on his head?

Frank!

. . . a woman with a toilet on her head?

Lu!

. . . a woman with two toilets on her head?

Lulu!

. . . a woman with a breeze on her head?

Gail!

. . . a woman with a tortoise on her head?

Shelley!

. . . a woman with a twig on her head?

Hazel!

. . . a man with a kilt on his head?

Scott!

. . . a man with a legal document on his head?

Will!

. . . a woman with a Christmas tree on her head?

Carol!

. . . a man with a Christmas tree on his head?

Noel!

. . . a man with a truck on his head?

Deceased!

. . . a man with some cat scratches?

Claude!

. . . a girl with one foot on each side of a river?

Bridget!

. . . a woman who climbs up walls?

Ivy!

. . . a man with rabbits in his pants?

Warren!

. . . a man who is always around when you need him?

Andy!

. . . a man floating in the sea?

Bob!

. . . a superhero that got run over by a steamroller?

Flatman!

. . . a Russian gardener?

Ivanhoe!

'Can't Sleep at Night'
by Constance Snoarer

'Chinese Lanterns'
by Eric Trician

'Confessions of a Thief'
by I Dunnit

'Falling from a Height'
by Eileen Toofar

'Maths for Beginners'
by Algy Brar

'Fighting off Burglars'
by Al Sayshun

'Housing Problem'
by Rufus Quick

'My Holiday with the Penguins'
by Anne Tarctic

'Pants Down'
by Lucy Lastic

'The Greediest Monster'
by Buster Gutt

'Foaming at the Mouth'
by Dee Monic

'In the Cannibal's Cauldron'
by Mandy Ceased

'My Crystal Ball'
by CA Lot

'A Time for Witch Hunting'
by Mae B Tomorrow

'The Long Sleep'
by Anna Sthetic

'The Rag and Bone Trade'
by Orson Cart

'Town Planning'
by Sir Veyor

'How to Keep Out a Vampire'
by Dora Steele

'My Life as a Jockey'
by Rhoda Horse

What will Bob the Builder be called when he retires?

Bob.

Person 1: 'Why are you wearing garlic around your neck?'

Person 2: 'It keeps away vampires.'

Person 1: 'But there aren't any vampires.'

Person 2: 'See, it works.'

A ghost walks into a bar.

Bartender: 'Sorry, we don't serve spirits here.'

Did you hear about the ghosts' race?

It was a dead heat.

Did you hear about the vampire comedian?

He specialised in biting satire.

Did you hear about the vampire who got taken away in a straightjacket?

He went batty.

Did you hear about the weather wizard?

He's forecasting sunny spells.

Do zombies like the dark?

Of corpse they do.

How can you tell if a corpse is angry?

It flips its lid.

What do you get if you cross a dinosaur with a vampire?

A blood shortage.

How can you tell what a ghost is getting for its birthday?

By feeling its presence.

How do you greet a three-headed monster?

'Hello, hello, hello.'

How do you make a witch itch?

Take away the W.

How does a yeti feel when it gets a cold?

Abominable.

How does Dracula eat his food?

In bite-sized pieces.

Police Officer 1: 'Where's the skeleton?'

Police Officer 2: 'I had to let him go.'

Police Officer 1: 'But he's our main suspect.'

Police Officer 2: 'I know. But I couldn't pin anything on him.'

What did Frankenstein do when he saw the monster catcher approaching?

He bolted.

What is Dracula's favourite fruit?

Necktarines!

What did the alien say to her son when he returned home?

'Where on Earth have you been?'

What did the alien say to the plant?

'Take me to your weeder.'

What is the first thing a monster does when you give him an axe?

Make out a chopping list.

What did the sea monster say when it saw the brand-new cruise ship sail past?

'Yum. Launch time.'

What do goblin children do after school?

Their gnomework.

What do little zombies play?

Corpse and robbers.

What do monsters have mid-morning?

A coffin break.

Why don't people kiss vampires?

Because they have bat breath.

What vehicles race at the Witches' Formula One Grand Prix?

Vroomsticks.

What do sea monsters eat?

Fish and ships.

What do vampires have for a snack?

Blood oranges.

What do you call a three-metre-long, two-headed monster?

Anything it wants.

What do you call a detective skeleton?

Sherlock Bones.

What do you call a ghost's mum and dad?

Transparents.

What do you call a hairy beast in a river?

A weir-wolf.

What do you call a witch without a broomstick?

A witch-hiker.

What do you do if you're surrounded by a witch, a werewolf, a vampire and two ghosts?

Hope you're at a costume party.

What does a monster say when introduced?

'Pleased to eat you.'

mmm,
breakfast!

Why should you never touch a monster's tail?

It's the end of the monster and the end of you.

What do you call a skeleton who sits around doing nothing?

Lazy bones.

What do zombies use to make cakes?

Self-raising flour.

What does a monster call his parents?

Dead and mummy.

What does a vampire never order at a restaurant?

Stake.

Why didn't the undertaker bury the skeleton?

He didn't have the guts.

How many monsters would it take to fill up your classroom?

I don't know. I wouldn't hang around to find out.

What happened to the naughty school witch?

She was ex-spelled.

What did the witch say to the vampire?

'Get a life!'

What happened when the gravediggers went on strike?

Their job was done by a skeleton crew.

What is a vampire's favourite sport?

Batminton.

What is a witch's favourite movie?

'Broom with a View.'

What is Dr. Jekyll's favourite game?

Hyde and seek.

What is Dracula's car called?

A blood mobile.

What is the favourite fair ride for little ghosts?

The rollerghoster.

What is the first part of a newspaper that a ghost turns to?

The horror-scope.

What did the ghost buy for his wife?

A see-through nightie.

What kind of plate does a skeleton eat off?

Bone china.

What kind of cheese do monsters eat?

Monsterella!

What song did the band play at the Demons and Ghouls ball?

'Demons are a Ghoul's Best Friend.'

What trees do ghosts like best?

Ceme-trees.

What type of music do mummies like best?

Ragtime.

What type of music do zombies like best?

Soul music.

What do ghosts use to type letters?

A type-frighter.

What was the skeleton rock band called?

The Strolling Bones.

What was the wizard's favourite band?

ABBA-cadabra.

What's a vampire's favourite dance?

The fangdango.

What don't zombies wear on boat trips?

Life jackets.

What's three metres tall, has twelve fingers, three eyes and wears sunglasses?

A monster on summer vacation.

What's a skeleton's favourite musical instrument?

A trom-bone.

Where do Australian ghosts live?

In the Northern Terror-tory.

Where do ghosts go swimming?

In the Dead Sea.

Which ghost is President of France?

Charles de Ghoul.

Who did the witch call when her broom was stolen?

The flying squad.

Who finished last at the Yeti Olympics?

Frosty the Slowman.

Why did Dracula take some medicine?

To stop his coffin.

First witch: 'My, hasn't your little girl grown!'

Second witch: 'Yes, she's certainly gruesome.'

Who is big and hairy, wears a dress and climbs the Empire State Building?

Queen Kong.

Who is King of the Cannibals?

Henry the Ate.

Who is the King of the Wizards?

William the Conjurer.

Who won the race between Count Dracula and Countess Dracula?

It was neck and neck.

Why are Cyclops couples happy together?

Because they always see eye to eye.

Why are ghosts always tired?

Because they are dead on their feet.

Why couldn't the witch race her horse in the Witches' Derby?

Because it was having a spell.

Why did the demon jump into the conserve?

Because he was a jammy devil.

Why do witches fly on broomsticks?

Because it's better than walking.

Why did the witches go on strike?

Because they wanted sweeping reforms.

Why did the executioner go to work early?

To get a head start.

Why did the vampire go to the orthodontist?

To improve his bite.

Why did the young vampire follow his dad's profession?

Because it was in his blood.

Why didn't the skeleton want to go to work?

Because his heart wasn't in it.

Why didn't the skeleton bother to defend itself in court?

Because it didn't have a leg to stand on.

Why do ghosts like the Spice Girls?

Because they're an all-ghoul band.

Why can ghosts speak Latin?

Because it's a dead language.

Why did the zombie decide to stay in his coffin?

He felt rotten.

Why do skeletons drink milk?

Because it's good for the bones.

Why do witches get good bargains?

Because they're good at haggling.

Why don't ghosts bother telling lies?

Because you can see right through them.

Why is Count Dracula skinny?

Because he eats necks to nothing.

Why isn't the Abominable Snowman scared of people?

Because he doesn't believe in them.

What do vampires cross the sea in?

Blood vessels.

What did King Kong say when his sister had a baby?

Well I'll be a monkey's uncle.

What happened when the Abominable Snowman ate hot pepper?

He melted.

What's green, sits in the corner and cries?

The Incredible Sulk.

What do you call a good-looking, kind and considerate monster?

A complete failure.

What do sea monsters eat for lunch?

Potato ships!

Why did the Cyclops give up teaching?

Because he only had one pupil.

What do Italian ghosts eat?

Spookgetti.

What do you call a sleeping monster who won't stay quiet?

Frankensnore.

What happened to Frankenstein's monster when he was caught speeding?

He was fined $50 and dismantled for six months.

What's a vampire's favourite dog?

A bloodhound!

What happened to the monster that took the five o'clock train home?

He had to give it back.

What do you get when you cross a vampire and a snowman?

Frostbite!

What do you get when you cross a skunk with Frankenstein?

Stinkenstein!

Which ghost ate the three bears' porridge?

Ghouldilocks.

What did the baby zombie want for his birthday?

A deady bear.

What did the vampire say when he had bitten someone?

'It's been nice gnawing you!'

What do you do with a green monster?

Put him in a paper bag till he ripens.

What is Dracula's favourite ice-cream flavour?

Vein-illa!

Why didn't the skeleton cross the road?

Because he didn't have the guts!

What do you call a lamb with a machine gun?

Lambo.

What did the alien say to the petrol pump?

Take your finger out of your ear when I'm talking to you.

Why don't turkeys get invited to dinner parties?

Because they use fowl language.

What do you get when you cross a rooster with a steer?

A cock and bull story.

What animal builds his house in the jungle?

A boa constructor.

What do you call an elephant that never washes?

A smellyphant.

What do you get if you cross a skunk with a bear?

Winnie the Poo.

What swings through the trees and is very dangerous?

A chimpanzee with a machine gun.

How did the skunk phone his mother?

On a smellular phone.

What do you call a group of people that dig for bones?

A skeleton crew.

What did the floor say to the desk?

I can see your drawers.

What's brown and sticky?

A stick.

What's the hardest part about skydiving?

The ground!

Why didn't the man die when he drank poison?

Because he was in the living room.

What do you get if you pour hot water down a rabbit hole?

Hot cross bunnies.

Why did the one-handed man cross the road?

He wanted to get to the secondhand shop!

What's a lion's favourite food?

Baked beings.

Mum: 'Haven't you finished filling the salt shaker yet?'

Son: 'Not yet. It's really hard to get the salt through all those little holes!'

John: 'Have you noticed your mother smells a bit funny these days?'

Will: 'No. Why?'

John: 'Well, your sister told me she was giving her a bottle of toilet water for her birthday!'

How did the dentist become a brain surgeon?

His drill slipped.

What did the undertaker say to his girlfriend?

'Em-balmy about you!'

What has four wheels and flies?

A garbage truck.

How do you make a Venetian blind?

Poke his eyes out.

Person 1: 'Pssst. Do you want to buy the genuine skull of Julius Caesar?'

Person 2: 'You sold me his skull last week. Besides, that one is smaller.'

Person 1: 'This is when he was a boy.'

Person 1: 'I've never been so insulted in all my life.'

Person 2: 'You haven't been trying.'

That dress fits you like a glove. It sticks out in five places.

The guy who invented the hokey-pokey died, but they couldn't get him into the coffin. His right leg was in, then his right leg was out, his right leg was . . .

When do you put a frog in your sister's bed?

When you can't find a mouse.

What happens when the Queen burps?

She issues a royal pardon.

What do you call a man with an elephant on his head?

Squashed.

What's the nearest thing to silver?

Lone Ranger's bottom.

A man went out for a walk and came across a little boy pulling his cat's tail.

'Hey you!' he shouted.
'Don't pull the cat's tail!'

'I'm not pulling,' replied the boy. 'I'm only holding on – the cat's doing the pulling!'

What goes in pink and comes out blue?

A swimmer on a cold day!

What did the royal taster say after drinking the poisoned water?

Not much!

What do well-behaved young lambs say to their mothers?

'Thank ewe!'